Jim Borgman's first drawing for the *Enquirer* appeared on the *Enquirer's* Sunday magazine cover for May 16, 1976. The drawing was one of six he made for a story about the value of Ohio to presidential candidates.

Jim's first cartoon for the *Enquirer's* editorial page appeared on Thursday, June 10, 1976, after President Gerald Ford won the Ohio Republican primary election.

JIM BORGMAN
My 25 Years at The Cincinnati Enquirer

J. DENNIS DOHERTY

Editor

RON HUFF

Designer

CONTENTS

Library of Congress Cataloging-in-Publication Data

All rights reserved. No part of this book may be used or reproduced in any manner whatsoever without written permission.

Library of Congress control number
2001096971

ISBN: 0-9630442-5-7

© *Copyright 2001* The Cincinnati Enquirer

Administrative and marketing direction by Martha L. Flanagan, assistant to the publisher of The Cincinnati Enquirer, *and by Gerald T. Silvers, vice president of marketing for the* Enquirer. *Drawings by Jim Borgman were picked by Jim and a jury of 27 Greater Cincinnatians. They are Betty Barnett, Ted Bergh, Sue Dance, Dennis Doherty, Mary Donaldson, Maureen Donohue, John Flanagan, Martha Flanagan, Gina Gardner, Carol Hahn, Shiela Holmes, Ron Huff, Vicki Jonas, Pam McFarland, Hoon Nam, Marianne Navin, Bruce Petrie Jr., David Preisser, Ed Rigaud, Barb Reid, Janette Rolcik, Nancy Rudig, Pat Runge, Gerald Silvers, Susan Smith, Jeff Suess and J.J. Wales.*

Technical assistance was provided by David E. Preisser, Enquirer *vice president of production.* Enquirer *employees Maureen Kelley, systems editor, and Tammy Robertson, publishing systems analyst, provided systems support. Advertising and marketing support was provided by Pam McFarland and Melinda Vonderahe of the* Enquirer's *Marketing Division. Photo support was provided by Charles Fry III, Steven M. Herppich and Michael E. Keating. Research assistance was provided by Ray Zwick,* Enquirer *librarian, and Sally Besten and Frank Harmon, assistant librarians.*

Copy editing was provided by Enquirer *news editor Beryl Love and deputy news editor Mark Ivancic and by the* Enquirer's *News Copy Desk: Paul Clark, David Herd, Bruce Holtgren, Barrett J. Brunsman, Phil Fisher, Gayle Brown, Carrie Ostermeyer, Jeff Williams, Amy Sutton, Cindi Andrews, Nikki Kingery, Sue Lancaster, Liz Pegram and Marty Hogan.*

This book was printed by the C.J. Krehbiel Co. on 80# Hanno-Art Silk stock. Text was set in 10.5 Garamond on an 11.5 point base. Some color drawings in this book were published originally in black and white. The color was added after publication for other published presentations.

INTRODUCTION

"Fresh from the Kenyon college newspaper, Jim Borgman was in my office being interviewed to succeed *Enquirer* editorial cartoonist legend L.D. Warren. His strength of purpose, character, intellect, humility and superb talent were so obvious, we knew immediately he would be an instant success. Personally and professionally, Jim has not only exceeded our fondest expectations, but in doing so he also has had a positive and lasting impact on our total community."

William J. Keating
Chairman, publisher, 1973-1984, 1990-1992

"Editorial cartoonists, by definition, are gunslingers, taking on everything and everyone. Jim Borgman was different. He made his opinions very clearly known, even if they didn't agree with the *Enquirer's* position. But most importantly, he did it with heart, compassion and humor. He could make you angry and smile. He could make you laugh and cry. All at the same time. This has always set him apart and will continue to do so."

Gary L. Watson
Publisher, 1984-1985

"Jim really cares about people and this community. He, like many at the *Enquirer*, works hard to make a difference in people's lives every day. He is not only a terrific cartoonist, he is a native son — a local treasure."

John P. Zanotti
Publisher, 1985-1990

"Jim Borgman is not only one of the nation's most talented cartoonists, but he also is one of the most likeable, thoughtful and approachable persons I know. *The Cincinnati Enquirer's* readers — those who agree with him and those who disagree — look forward to Jim's wit, intelligence and insight whenever they open our newspaper. He is recognized for his excellence by his peers and he is appreciated as one of Cincinnati's treasured citizens."

Harry M. Whipple
Publisher

This book is the culmination of *The Cincinnati Enquirer's* celebration of Jim Borgman's silver anniversary at the newspaper. It introduces readers to Jim in a friendly and intimate way. Much of the biographical information comes from interviews with Jim's family — a sister, his mother — including a chapter written by his son and daughter. Jim and his mother opened the family archives and provided the family photos, which appear in the biographical chapters. Jim's *Enquirer* family contributes most of the text, and his partner in the *Zits* comic strip, Jerry Scott, gives you the inside story on how the strip began.

And the book is loaded with Borgman drawings, each with commentary by Jim. You revisit the 10 that won a Pulitzer Prize. Jim picks his favorite 25 cartoons. And a diverse jury of 27 Greater Cincinnatians — some *Enquirer* employees, some not — picks the remainder. There are 126 "Best of Borgman" drawings in these 208 pages.

Eleven of Jim's professional colleagues — each acclaimed as one of America's top artists or cartoonists — submitted caricatures of Jim. Each reveals the deep respect and appreciation they have for him.

Our wish is that you come to know Jim better through this salute to his illustrious career at *The Cincinnati Enquirer*.

Ward Bushee
Editor

THE PRIZE: HIGH HONOR FOR A HOMETOWN HERO

BY JOHN KIESEWETTER

Enquirer radio and television critic John Kiesewetter joined the newspaper a year before Jim Borgman. They met at an Easter egg hunt for children of the news staff.

While the champagne flowed on the fifth floor of the *Enquirer* building, the fax machine in Jim Borgman's tiny third-floor office overflowed with a steady stream of congratulatory messages from his cartoonist colleagues.

On the afternoon of Tuesday, April 9, 1991, Jim learned that he had won journalism's top award for editorial cartoonists.

After 15 years at *The Cincinnati Enquirer*, the 37-year-old Price Hill native had snagged the big one, the 1991 Pulitzer Prize for Editorial Cartooning.

The "April Agonies," as he called them, were over. It had been six years since he had first learned he was a finalist for the Pulitzer, awarded annually by Columbia University. And for six years or more, cartoonist pals like Mike Peters of the *Dayton Daily News* had been telling Jim that his day would come.

"Editorial cartoonists are a small, close-knit group, maybe only about 200 of us," Jim explained that day in 1991. "As soon as you achieve any notoriety, people start saying, 'You're going to win the Pulitzer soon, wait and see.'

"Once people start saying that, the anticipation starts building every year so much you can't rest in April, knowing the announcement's coming. It's the April agonies."

The timing for the prize was extra special for Publisher and Chairman William J. Keating and Editor and Vice President George Blake: News of Jim's Pulitzer would be published the next morning in the 150th anniversary edition of the *Enquirer*.

At the fifth-floor reception that day, while surrounded by his wife, Lynn, and their children, Dylan, 8, and Chelsea, 16 months, Jim thanked his family for helping win the awards. He thanked his friends. In fact, he thanked the entire city of Cincinnati.

This wasn't just nice-guy Jim Borgman being the polite, thoughtful person that he is. He really meant it.

Cincinnati had given him a wealth of news stories in 1990

A representative of the Pulitzer Prize Board called Jim on the afternoon of April 9, 1991, to tell him he had won the prize for editorial cartooning.
Enquirer photographer Gary Landers was with Jim and made this photo as he received the news.

that made national headlines, such as the criminal obscenity charges against the Contemporary Arts Center for exhibiting Robert Mapplethorpe's "The Perfect Moment" photos and Cincinnati Bengals coach Sam Wyche banning female reporters from the team locker room.

These were in his prize-winning folio, along with cartoons about the end of communism in the Soviet Union, the reunification of Germany, the national savings and loan crisis, the postal rate hike, increasing Mideast tensions building up to the Gulf War (in early 1991), the AIDS death of Indiana teen-ager Ryan White, and President George Bush backpedaling from his "Read my lips: no new taxes" campaign promise.

His friends and family played a major role in the Pulitzer by helping him select the final 10 entries from some 60 to 80 cartoons.

"I got to the point where I thought, well, maybe I'm not the best judge of my own work," he explained in a conversation while preparing this book.

"You get to where you like a certain cartoon because you

Columbia University
in the City of New York

NEW YORK, N.Y. 10027

PRESIDENT'S ROOM

April 9, 1991

Dear Mr. Borgman:

I am delighted to confirm the award to you of the 1991 Pulitzer Prize for Editorial Cartooning. It is also my pleasure on behalf of the Pulitzer Prize Board to invite you and a personal guest to a ceremony and reception here at Columbia commemorating the 75th anniversary of the Pulitzer Prizes, at which we will present this year's Prize winners with their checks and Certificates of Award.

The anniversary event, to which all living Prize winners will be invited and which we intend as a congenial celebration of achievement, will be held on September 22nd on the Columbia campus. You will receive a more formal invitation to this affair in due course, but if you can attend, I would appreciate your writing Mr. Robert Christopher (c/o Pulitzer Prize Office, 702 Journalism, Columbia University) to notify him of that fact and to indicate whether or not you will bring a guest. If you cannot be with us, your Certificate of Award and $3,000 check will, of course, be mailed to you.

Please accept my warmest congratulations on an outstanding achievement. I hope I shall have the pleasure of greeting you personally on September 22nd.

Sincerely,

Michael I. Sovern

Dear Mr. Borgman:

I am delighted to confirm the award to you of the 1991 Pulitzer Prize for Editorial Cartooning. It is also my pleasure on behalf of the Pulitzer Prize Board to invite you and a personal guest to a ceremony and reception here at

finally captured a guy's likeness, or you like the way you drew the hand. You see something different from what other people see. I thought it might be helpful to have some outside eyes look at them. So I'd spread the cartoons out when friends came over."

He had a feeling back then that 1991 could be his year.

"A lot of things were happening in Cincinnati that year, and it felt to me that forces were converging. There was a feeling of karma to it. The eyes of the country had focused on Cincinnati for these various dubious reasons. I had tried to rise to those occasions," he said.

Jim, who often works late into the night at his home studio while listening to Cincinnati Reds games on the radio, talks about his Hall of Fame season in baseball terms.

"I was hitting them as well as I knew how to hit. I was seeing the ball, as Tony Perez would say," referring to the Reds' former first baseman and batting coach. "The way I remember it, it was a year of real clarity for me. Maybe like the way Roger Maris looked back on the season of '61 (when he broke Babe Ruth's home-run record). You could tell you were at your best, there was

The letter at right is the formal notification of the award of the prize by the Pulitzer Prize Board at Columbia University. The formal program for the award ceremony on Sept. 22, 1991, (far right) adds Jim's name to the distinguished list of previous winners.

a great flow going. I was just in a real groove."

His Pulitzer-winning entry, reprinted on these pages, is a testament to Jim's impressive versatility, a source of great admiration by his fellow cartoonists. While many cartoonists stick to a single style, Jim draws on a wide variety of tools.

A Borgman cartoon can be as simple as an angel in heaven hugging little Ryan White. (Ryan's mom loved it so much she had the cartoon etched into Ryan's grave marker.) Or a Borgman cartoon can be as complex as an eight-panel skewering of people bellyaching about the new 30-cent first-class stamp.

He nailed President George Bush for breaking his no-tax pledge by spoofing the fine print on new car advertisements — with a hilarious 258-word text that still makes people laugh out loud when Jim reads it at speaking appearances.

In contrast, his comment about the fall of communism — circles of dominoes about to topple Soviet President Mikhail S. Gorbachev — didn't say one word. Another one about the Soviet collapse in this collection

takes an entirely different approach, a *New Yorker*-style cartoon about a plump, middle-class homeowner — an image now familiar to Borgman fans — declaring to his wife: "Now that communism is dead, I think I'll take a nap."

THE PULITZER PRIZES

1985	JEFF MACNELLY of the *Chicago Tribune*.
1986	JULES FEIFFER of *The Village Voice*, New York City.
1987	BERKE BREATHED of *The Washington Post* Writers Group.
1988	DOUG MARLETTE of *The Atlanta Constitution* and *The Charlotte Observer*.
1989	JACK HIGGINS of the *Chicago Sun-Times*.
1990	TOM TOLES of *The Buffalo News* for his work during the year as exemplified by the cartoon "First Amendment."
1991	JIM BORGMAN of *The Cincinnati Enquirer*.

1917-1991

COLUMBIA UNIVERSITY IN THE
CITY OF NEW YORK

The two communism cartoons are among his favorites for different reasons. The classic-style Gorbachev illustration was one of just a handful he has produced without any labels or captions — although that always has been Jim's goal when putting

a pencil to paper.

"I've always had this thing about not wanting to be just a punch line writer that you tack a drawing to. I've always said: I don't want to do the kind of cartoons that Jay Leno or Johnny Carson could have said in a monologue, when you just take a funny joke, and put a picture on it," said Jim, who frequently watches David Letterman's "Late Night" or Ted Koppel's "Nightline" (more than Leno's "Tonight Show") while working late in his home studio. He also consumes large daily doses of public radio (Morning Edition, All Things Considered, Terry Gross, Diane Rehm) and TV's all-news channels.

"To me, the essence of cartooning is letting the visuals tell the story," he said. "It's just my particular code that I try to be as visual as I can in my work."

The overweight man stuffed into the overstuffed chair talking about the end of communism in 1990 was one of the first of what would become a frequent source for Borgman commentary. His fellow cartoonists credit Jim with discovering this radical new forum for political/social commentary, taking issues

"The way I remember it, it was a year of real clarity for me. Maybe like the way Roger Maris looked back on the season of '61 (when he broke Babe Ruth's home-run record). You could tell you were at your best, there was a great flow going. I was just in a real groove."

Jim Borgman

literally right into newspaper readers' living rooms.

With the validation of a Pulitzer, he did more and more drawings with these "big doughy people in their house talking about issues — average Ohioans dealing with issues as they filter down into everyday life," he said.

"This was a new place for editorial cartoons. Editorial cartoonists will tell you that's sort of my contribution to the field — finding cartoons where you didn't used to look for them, scenes with real people. The kind of people you and I grew up with. They're the kind of scenes I've always lived my life around," said Jim, who grew up in the working-class neighborhood of Price Hill, the son of a commercial artist. His mom, Marian, still lives in the two-story brick house.

"I think it's kind of like Bruce Springsteen writing about New Jersey: It has this universal appeal. Everybody sort of finds their own world in it," he said. "I've come to love doing cartoons this way."

His pal Mike Peters and other cartoonists marveled at Jim's ability to think outside the box. While most editorial cartoonists scrutinized the front pages and wire stories scrambling for inspiration during slow news periods, Jim put down the paper

Celebration of Jim's Pulitzer Prize extended beyond the Enquirer. He was invited to address Cincinnati City Council. With him are son, Dylan, wife, Lynn, and mother, Marian.

and looked at life. Peters thought Jim's 1993 cartoon about the stress of last-minute Christmas shoppers ("A Mall and the Night Visitors") was pure genius.

"He observed life around him, and did social commentaries that were amazing," said Peters, who won the 1981 Pulitzer. "I had never seen anything like it before. Boy, did he teach me something: That if nothing is going on, you don't have to be tied to the front page."

Behind every truly great cartoon burns a cartoonist's passion. That was the case with Jim's prize-winners about Ryan White's AIDS death and the attempt by Cincinnati authorities to censor the Mapplethorpe photo exhibit. A drawing of Sheriff Simon Leis hauling in Michelangelo's sculpture of David — "Your Honor, we found this clown parading around naked in a homoerotic pose" — was one of his many Mapplethorpe cartoons. (The CAC and Director Dennis Barrie were indicted in April 1990 for pandering obscenity and illegal use of a child in nudity-related material for Mapplethorpe's photo show. They were acquitted on all charges six months later.)

"Mapplethorpe merited lots of commentary, and I knew

how I stood from the very beginning," he said. "I could see what people felt was offensive about it, but to me it was clear that you can't shut a city down around things like that. People should see what they want to see. We're all grown-ups. Art isn't always pretty. So I felt good. It was almost like a campaign of mine to talk about it.

"On this occasion, I just had the idea and wanted to get it down. It was just so clear to me how to do it that I just drew it without bothering to do a rough."

Jim found the Pulitzer to be liberating, and not just from the annual April Agonies. He compares it to getting an A on a final report card. He had passed the class; now he was free to experiment. He believes — and his loyal readers will agree — that his work has improved in the past decade. In fact, a majority of cartoons in this book were published after the Pulitzer.

"The glory of the Pulitzer is that once you get it, you don't have to worry about it any more. That was the best gift to me," he said. "I felt it gave me permission to explore, to be adventurous, and to be more and more myself. I could argue that the work since it has been better than the work before."

"He observed life around him, and did social commentaries that were amazing. I had never seen anything like it before. Boy, did he teach me something: That if nothing is going on, you don't have to be tied to the front page."

Mike Peters

Others concur. He won the National Headliner Award in 1991, and his second Sigma Delta Chi Award in 1995. (The first was in 1978.) The National Cartoonists Society honored him as best editorial cartoonist for a fourth time in 1994 (in addition to his 1987-88-89 streak), and presented him the Reuben Award (named for Rube Goldberg) for being the most outstanding of all editorial, comic strip and animation cartoonists in 1993.

Also in 1993, he found himself in the Oval Office during the first two months of the young Clinton administration. President Clinton had invited eight cartoonists and their wives to an informal Saturday get-together. The select company included Pulitzer winners Jeff MacNelly (*Chicago Tribune*), Mike Peters (*Dayton Daily News*), Tony Auth (*Philadelphia Inquirer*), Herb Block (*Washington Post*), Doug Marlette (*New York Newsday*) and legendary Warner Bros. animator Chuck Jones.

As they were introducing themselves, the president shocked Jim by announcing, "I know you. I have one of your cartoons hanging in my bathroom."

He proceeded to lead Jim down a little windowless hallway between his study and the Oval Office, the windowless hallway that would become infamous as

25 PEOPLE WHO CRACK ME UP

Dave Barry
Wayne Brady
David Letterman
Tom and Ray Magliozzi
David Sedaris
Bob Beemon
Laura Pulfer
Jim Carrey
Jerry Scott
Ben Stiller
Mike Peters
Jean Shepherd
The Simpsons
Billy Crystal
Jack Handey
Steven Wright
Garrison Keillor
James Thurber
Dennis Miller
Leslie Nielsen
Mike Peters
Nicole Sullivan
Conan O'Brien
Michael Richards
Dan Quayle

the site of one of Clinton's trysts with intern Monica Lewinsky. Above the toilet was a framed Borgman cartoon from the 1992 campaign. It showed a doctor holding a stethoscope to a discombobulated Clinton while telling a Democratic donkey: "He's still breathing . . .

looks like he's our nominee."

The cartoon never was one of Jim's particular favorites, but it appealed to the "Comeback Kid" part of the former Arkansas governor's ego. And of all the Pulitzer winners summoned by President Clinton that day, the only cartoonist whose work was displayed anywhere in the Oval Office area was by Jim — even if it was literally bathroom humor.

"It was really cool," Jim said. "I guess it's sort of like the anti-Pulitzer, getting your cartoon on Clinton's bathroom wall. Both are honors — in very different ways."

May 20, 1990
This was drawn when George Bush began to back away from his "no new taxes" pledge.
I racked my brain for all the disclaimers I'd ever read.

"NOW THAT COMMUNISM IS DEAD, I THINK I'LL TAKE A NAP."

February 4, 1990
Some cartoons are surgical strikes on specific items in the news. This one, though, was a broad,
loopy comment that seemed to capture the relief at the end of the Cold War.

April 12, 1990
The Mapplethorpe exhibit had Cincinnatians talking about things heretofore unmentionable in polite company.
This may well be the only time male frontal nudity made it into the pages of *The Cincinnati Enquirer*.

January 30, 1990
Gorbachev made it easy for cartoonists by providing his own identifying label on his forehead.
Though the Pulitzer Prize is awarded for a portfolio of work, this is the drawing most often cited from the entries.

"ACTUALLY, IT'S SO WE ALWAYS KNOW WHERE THEY ARE."

September 30, 1990
German reunification, though welcome in most quarters, nonetheless
set off silent alarms for those who remembered the world wars.

October 7, 1990
Coach Sam Wyche threw three female reporters out of the Bengals
locker room in a classic case of misdirected frustration.

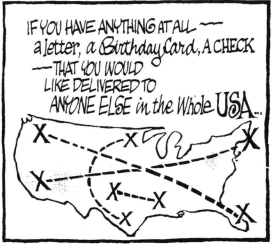

March 11, 1990
It's so easy to slam the U.S. Postal Service, and I've done my share. This time, the whining over
a 1-cent postage increase seemed silly, and I challenged myself to defend the service.

A PLACE WHERE NO ONE IS AFRAID TO HUG

April 10, 1990
A decade after Ryan White's death, this drawing is the one most recalled by people talking about my work.
It is engraved on Ryan's grave marker and has been sampled on hundreds of squares on the AIDS quilt.

September 3, 1990
Before the Gulf War erupted, President Bush led a world blockade of Iraq,
hoping to bring Saddam Hussein to his knees. It was slow going.

June 24, 1990
Our own Home State fiasco was a local manifestation of a bigger national savings and loan crisis.

HOW DID JIM BORGMAN GET FROM THERE TO HERE?

Five-year-old Jim Borgman had a smile for his kindergarten picture from Carson Elementary School in Price Hill in 1959. He had a bigger smile on April 9, 1991, as *Enquirer* executives saluted him and his family (wife, Lynn, daughter, Chelsea, and son, Dylan) on his Pulitzer Prize. The *Enquirer* executives are, from left, James Schwartz, vice president of finance, James Deavy, vice president of human resources, and George Blake, editor and vice president. Behind Mr. Blake is Cindy Fangman, secretary to the publisher. The following chapters tell how Jim made the journey from childhood to the pinnacle of his profession.

This Very Vanilla Lad Is No Lord Fauntleroy

By Laura Pulfer

Enquirer Metro columnist Laura Pulfer is featured frequently on National Public Radio. A veteran journalist and book author, she thought she could discover a few early skeletons in the Borgman cupboards but found the cupboards bare.

He got a perfect start in life.

James Mark Borgman, future Pulitzer Prize-winning cartoonist, was born Wednesday, Feb. 24, 1954, at Good Samaritan Hospital in Cincinnati. He thoughtfully arrived at 4:50 in the afternoon, allowing his parents, Jim and Marian, a good night's sleep on the eve of their first son's birth. His eyes were blue, his hair was light brown and his head was round. His mother pronounced him a "darling baby boy."

He walked when he was supposed to, ate solid foods on schedule. He spoke when bidden, did not play with matches, did not throw tantrums, served as an altar boy at St. William Church. He played quietly with a Slinky and toy soldiers. He wore Davy Crockett boots and a cowboy hat.

He contracted chicken pox, measles and mumps. "Mild cases," his mother says proudly.

His kindergarten teacher, Mrs. Mooney, pronounced him "very capable."

This was one relentlessly darling boy. At least according to his mother.

Generally speaking, if you want the dirt on a guy, you can usually count on his sister. Mary Jo Borgman tries to be helpful. "I'm sorry. I just can't remember anything but good. He was so vanilla, so quiet. He never got into trouble. He was just the hero of the family."

The Borgmans outgrew their little two-bedroom house on Clearview Avenue in Price Hill, moving to a bigger one on Trenton Avenue when Jim was 8. By then, Jim and his older sisters, Mary Jo and Kathy, had been joined by the youngest boy, Tom. Permission was given for the Borgman children to continue at St. William, although technically they were in another parish.

Loyal. Traditional. Catholic.

"We were such a functional family," Jim remembers. "Dinner together every night. We talked about what we'd done that day. It was the healthiest kind of sharing. I never doubted that everybody would be around the dinner table. A wonderful sense of security, stability."

His record at St. William Elementary was excellent. His first-grade teacher, Sister Laura Ann, notified his parents that the boy "has a definite artistic talent, prints letters very well." But another teacher warned later that he should stop fooling with cartoons and do something more productive.

The customarily obedient boy ignored her.

"He was always sketching," Marian says.

Jim's dad was a commercial artist, a sign painter. "There were always art supplies around the house," Jim says, "giving me unspoken permission to do it. I always knew art was my thing, that I could draw."

And it would be altogether understandable if he wanted to be like his father. "He was the center of the family," Jim says. "He brought us up to think about our world and challenge it."

Summers were the best. Mr. Borgman worked at night, in the garage. At bedtime, Jim

would head downstairs in his pajamas to say good night to his father. The big garage door

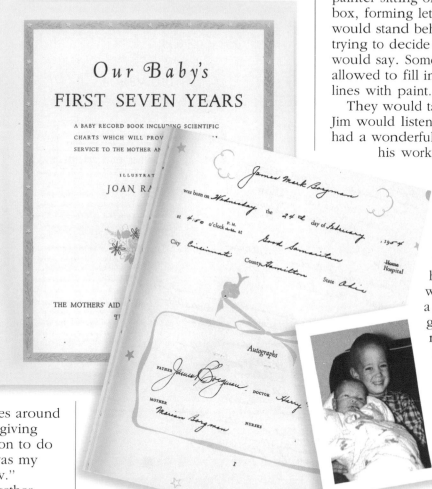

stood open. Waite Hoyt calling Reds games on the radio. Crickets outside. The sign painter sitting on a wooden box, forming letters. The boy would stand behind his father, trying to decide what the sign would say. Sometimes he was allowed to fill in the chalked lines with paint.

They would talk. Or, rather, Jim would listen to his dad. "He had a wonderful way of making his work life sound like a giant soap opera. He was a very 'present' father, very involved with us." But a homebody. It was Jim's uncle, a priest, who gave him a notion that he might have access to a world outside his neighborhood. Father Gene Maly was "very worldly in a way we were not," Jim says. He traveled, went to the Second Vatican Council, "sent us the subconscious message that you could go from

Three years after Jim was born on February 24, 1954, he found himself holding his new brother Tom. Each wound up in the newspaper business; Tom is creative director of features for the *St. Louis Post-Dispatch*.

The Borgman children in 1958 (from left): Kathy, Mary Jo, Tom and Jim.

MY 25 FAVORITE PLACES

Santa Fe, NM
San Francisco, CA
Chautauqua, NY
Maui, HI
Florence, Italy
Florence, KY
Flint Hill, VA
Price Hill
Abiquiui, NM
Jamestown, ND
(home of the world's largest buffalo)
Grand Canyon
Juneau, AK
Glacier National Park, MT
Gambier, OH
Sarasota, FL
Ann Arbor, MI
Helsinki, Finland
Amsterdam, Netherlands
Chicago, IL
Arches National Park, UT
New Orleans, LA
Outer Banks, NC
Meeteetsee, WY
Pittsburgh, PA
Barrow, AK

Price Hill to anywhere."

And there were books, starting with Golden Books and leading up to more complicated fare. "He read a lot," Marian says.

When he finished one by Kurt Vonnegut Jr., he wrote a fan letter. The author replied. The boy framed the letter. At the end of every school year, used textbooks were sold off. In the fifth grade, Jim bought a history book. And spent the summer reading and *outlining* it.

"That was his summer project," Mary Jo marvels. "I'm sorry. He was just a really, really good kid."

Kind of a goody-goody?

Not at all, according to Wayne Laib, whose backyard ran into the Borgmans' on Trenton Avenue. "He was fun. We had fun. Camped out in the backyard, played baseball and football."

Jim was first baseman, using an Orlando Cepeda glove. He also named his bicycle after the San Francisco Giants player. "San Francisco just seemed so exotic to me," Jim says.

They were intrigued by a retired baseball player who

lived in the neighborhood, John "Root Beer" Pramesa.

And Jim became even more intrigued by Wayne's sister, Carol. "They used to hold hands under the card table," Wayne remembers.

"Cartooning was a way to make connections with girls," Jim says. "I couldn't talk to them, couldn't dance."

He copied pictures of teen idols from magazines, painstakingly shading and sketching their faces. Carol loved the Monkees. "I spent hours and hours on these drawings for her," he says.

Years later, a stranger called to say she had some drawings with his signature. Pictures of teen-age heartthrobs from the '60s. They were Jim's. Carol had been selling them on the playground for a quarter.

Jim laughs. A nice, high-pitched hoot. When he is thoroughly amused, it's a little bit like the sound somebody makes going down the first hill of a roller coaster. A practiced listener, not the life of the party, Jim spills his wit onto paper. He's friendly, but not really comfortable, even now, in big groups.

"I don't know what to do

Jim and his younger brother Tom visit Santa in 1962, and they greet an Easter character in 1963 in a costume designed by their dad.

with people, except to observe them."

The Borgmans and their large, extended family — brothers and sisters and spouses and kids — vacation together every year at the Outer Banks in North Carolina. "Jim spends a lot of time on the couch, in the middle of things," Mary Jo says, "but not always participating.

Jim's seventh grade report card from St. William School was no fluke. He was an A student through college. He donned his Cub Scout uniform for his ninth birthday in 1963.

EXPLANATION OF MARKS

A—93-100 Superior
B—85-92 Above Average
C—77-84 Average—Work done on grade level

D—70-76 Below Average
E—65-69 Condition
F—Below 65 Failure

PERIODS	1	2	Exam.	3	4	Exam.	Year's Aver.
Religion	a	a	98	a-	B	89	a-
Reading	a	a	95	a	a	92	a
English Oral and Written	a	a	95	a-	B	97	a-
Spelling	a	a	100	a	a	99	a
Arithmetic	a	a	93	a	a	97	a
Social Studies Geography, History, Civics	a	a-	100	a-	a	87	a
Writing	B	B					
Science — Health — Safety	a	a	95				
Art	a	a					
Music	B						
ATTENDANCE Days Absent	—	—					
Times Tardy							

NOTE: Promotion is based upon grades received in Spelling, Arithmetic, and Social Studies.

Freedom Means To Me

according to Webster's ...te Dictionary, is "exemp- necessity in choice and ...ly it is this, but freedom ...re to me.

He's pensive, thoughtful."

Jim says it's one of the things he misses most about his childhood, about those years spent in Price Hill. Everybody — his mom, his sisters, his friends — remembers the bag of plastic men and animals Jim hauled around when he was little. "He could play with them for hours," his mother says.

"What I was doing was daydreaming," he says. Making elaborate zoos for the animals. Imagining the men in communities, in stores, in families. "Daydreaming. That's where all the good stuff

A SALUTE FROM A COLLEAGUE

Several of Jim's professional colleagues were asked to commemorate his silver anniversary at The Enquirer. *This drawing was created by Mike Peters, Pulitzer Prize winning cartoonist for the Dayton Daily News.*

NEANDERTHAL MAN

JAVA MAN

PEKING MAN

BORGMAN

©2001 MIKE PETERS

happens. In your childhood, you have a lot of time to just think."

He says when he was sick, his mother could get him to stay quiet by handing him a piece of construction paper and some scissors.

"What's in my head has always seemed very rich. That's where everything comes from."

Well, from that. And from the nights in the garage. And the hundreds — no, thousands —

of hours around the dinner table. From the nuns at St. William. From his peripatetic uncle. From his decidedly functional family.

Didn't he ever get in real trouble?

"Nope," says Mary Jo. Rebellion?

"He and Tom painted their room black."

Aha.

"They had permission."

How about that room? Messy?

"He was neat. Sorry."

No visits to the principal's office?

"I'm very sorry," his sister says sincerely.

Jim Borgman — the little boy who quietly arranged plastic men, imagining a story for them, who learned to examine the outside world in the comfortable circle of an approving family — probably can't be blamed for his dependable decency.

After all, he got a perfect start.

Portrait of the Writer as a Young Artist

By John Johnston

Enquirer *feature writer John Johnston grew up in Coshocton, Ohio, not far from Kenyon College, where Jim Borgman attended college.*

Jim Borgman entered high school at the height of the psychedelic '60s, a turbulent time when drugs, protests and rebellious youth tore at the very fabric of American society.

Jim's contribution to the anti-establishment movement: He once drew a cartoon of his high school's assistant principal with a *hairy wart on his nose.*

If you can imagine.

"You have to remember we were in Price Hill," Jim says, "so it seemed really about 1958."

Fast-forward to his college years, and another startling revelation: One time during senior year — and only one time — Jim and his best friend patronized a campus bar, *and they drank too much.*

A picture begins to emerge of Jim Borgman's high school and college years. It is not a picture of a wild-and-crazy guy.

"Has anyone given you anything, besides that he was a good student and a good boy?" asks Chris Myers, the aforementioned best friend.

Well, no.

Not that we went looking to dig up dirt, mind you. It's just that, when poking around into a person's past — especially the teen years — you figure a few unflattering stories might surface.

OK, there's this: In high school, Jim went downtown to see *Midnight Cowboy*, the X-rated Academy Award winner, *without his parents' permission.*

Ooooh.

Aside from that, what you hear are comments like this: "He was pretty much the golden boy. Whatever he touched always turned out extremely well." That's from Mark Wiesner, a classmate of Jim's at Elder High School, which is where this story begins.

There was never much doubt Jim would attend the all-boys high school at Vincent and Regina avenues. His Roman Catholic elementary school, St. William, fed into Elder. It was that simple.

As a freshman in the fall of 1968, Jim walked into the Gothic brick tower that serves as the school's main entrance and immediately gravitated toward

Writer's digest

22 East Twelfth Street, Cincinnati, Ohio 45210, Phone 513/241-0710

August 17, 1970

James M. Borgman
541 Trenton Avenue
Cincinnati, Ohio 45238

Dear Mr. Borgman

Re: ONLY A YOUNG MAN

Congratulations! Your manuscript has won 71st prize in the Short
Story category of our 1970 Creative Writing Awards Contest.

Would you be kind enough to send us both background information on
your prize-winning entry, and a short biographical sketch highlighting
your writing credits and experience.

If you would like us to forward a publicity release to your local
newspaper, please send us its name and address. And please let me
know when and to whom you sell your prize-winning manuscript.

Cordially,

Richard Rosenthal

Richard Rosenthal
Publisher

RR/dp

Enclosure

"the art guys and the eggheads," he says.

"I'm sort of ashamed to say that I was a very good student. I wasn't the class clown, that kind of guy. I wish I had those credentials."

He took school seriously. He worked hard, earned good grades.

"I always liked writing, and literature, art. I just threw myself into it. I loved it all. I still do."

If in high school Jim was, as he says, "always just a little too straight," then art was a way to warp — however slightly — that G-rated image.

By then he had discovered *Mad* magazine, which featured work by artists such as Mort Drucker and Jack Davis. He emulated their style in the caricatures of teachers he was always drawing in the margins of notebooks.

His drawings found a slightly larger audience his sophomore year when, with the blessing of English teacher Charlie Hotchkiss, a small group of students launched the *Giraffe*. "It was, at Elder, the closest you could come to an underground publication," he says. Which of course was not close at all.

The holiday edition featured a takeoff on "The Twelve Days of Christmas." But something was missing: Jim's censored drawing of "eight maids a-milking."

Jim's early artistic aspirations were literary. Despite a 71st prize in a creative writing competition, he pursued writing as a career goal through his first two years of college.

Jim and Kathy Thompson, a Mount St. Joseph College student, won second place in the 1974 banner contest sponsored by the Reds. The press release from the Reds reveals that Jim has changed his career goal to editorial cartooning. Right are Jim's original sketches of Sparky Anderson, Pete Rose and Dave Concepcion for the banner, which was painted in enamel on oil cloth.

"The eight maids a-milking had been our assistant principal milking the student body," Jim says. "He had just raised the price of milk in the cafeteria.

"I remember that being the first time I kind of got in official trouble over a cartoon. I think that's where I got my first taste of the thrill and danger of playing this (cartooning) game. In the little world I occupied, that was an uncharacteristic brush with authority."

Cartooning could be fun, all right, but it didn't figure into his career aspirations. Jim wanted to be a writer.

His love for literature led him to works by Steinbeck, Faulkner, Hemingway, Joyce Carol Oates. A class assignment turned him on to Kurt Vonnegut Jr. Then one day Hotchkiss, the English teacher, found Vonnegut's phone number and called him up during class.

"We were all astonished," Jim says.

The resulting interview was published in the *Giraffe*, along with a Borgman drawing of Vonnegut.

Jim sent the famous author his drawing, with a letter saying he wanted to be a novelist.

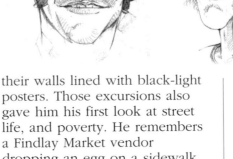

Vonnegut wrote back, telling of a friend who had a sign in her studio. It said, "You can do anything if you just begin."

In his high school years, Jim was just beginning to get a glimpse at the world beyond Price Hill.

He and friends sometimes rode a bus downtown. They'd walk up Vine Street, peeking in head shops laden with incense, their walls lined with black-light posters. Those excursions also gave him his first look at street life, and poverty. He remembers a Findlay Market vendor dropping an egg on a sidewalk, and a homeless man picking it up and devouring it.

His summer job was an eye-opener, too. In high school and college, he worked in a Lower Price Hill shop where workers painted signs on the sides of beverage trucks, moving vans and the like. It was a gritty place, managed by his father, with diesel fumes and spray paint odors and alcoholics wandering in from Eighth and State to bum money.

The National Honor Society student found himself among an interesting cast of characters: a man who took home the shop's wooden soda-pop crates so he could build a house; a worker, known to have killed a man, who showed up with a gun one day and threatened the foreman; and an assortment of unskilled laborers who hit the neighborhood bar every payday.

Working alongside them was part of growing up. So, too, was facing some hard realities.

One day after school, Jim and his brother learned from their mother that a next-door neighbor, George Beale, had been killed in Vietnam.

"We were out in the backyard, shooting baskets, trying to process that. And his two brothers came home from school, through our backyard. They stopped and shot baskets with us for a half-hour before they went into the house. We were just paralyzed, not knowing what the hell to do.

"That's as close as Vietnam

came to my personal life."

Jim turned 18 in February 1972. No new draft orders were issued after that year, and the withdrawal of U.S. servicemen from Vietnam was well under way. Still, he felt it important for his convictions to be known. So he applied for, and was granted, conscientious objector status.

Early his senior year, he was recognized at Elder's honors convocation for having the highest grade average as a junior: 97 percent. He told the student newspaper: "Art is very definitely a part of my life. I'm not out to win outstanding awards in art. I merely wish to improve my talent for my own personal satisfaction."

When it came time to choose a college, Jim considered Notre Dame and St. John's. But he visited only one campus: Kenyon College, a picturesque school atop a hill in the central Ohio town of Gambier.

Still planning to be a writer, Jim was drawn to Kenyon by its

CINCINNATI REDS NEWS RELEASE

for further information, please contact jim ferguson,
100 riverfront stadium, cincinnati, ohio 45202
phone (513) 421-4510

FOR IMMEDIATE RELEASE

Banner Day Feature

CINCINNATI, Ohio -- Jim Borgman of Cincinnati wants to be an editorial cartoonist someday and for the past three years has used the Cincinnati Reds-sponsored Banner Day at Riverfront Stadium to prepare him for his future endeavor.

English department, which had been made famous by the likes of poet Robert Lowell and John Crowe Ransom. The latter had founded the *Kenyon Review,* an important literary journal.

Once on campus in the fall of '72, it didn't take Jim long to find the art department.

That's where he met professor Martin John Garhart, a South Dakotan as rugged and imposing as the Black Hills. To the kid from Cincinnati, he looked "scary as hell."

"The first time I saw him," Jim says, "I thought, just stay away from this guy. But he could draw like an angel. I just wanted to learn everything I could from him."

Learn he did. Garhart became Jim's most important teacher.

"I remember that being the first time I kind of got in official trouble over a cartoon. I think that's where I got my first taste of the thrill and danger of playing this (cartooning) game. In the little world I occupied, that was an uncharacteristic brush with authority."

Jim Borgman

Far right, at Elder High School, Jim probed the patience of authority by caricaturing the principal of Seton High School and faculty members of Elder.

"The thing about Jim that sets him apart from most human beings is that he is focused, he has a great deal of discipline, and he cares," says Garhart, who still teaches at Kenyon. "He cares about people. He thinks that life can actually be better. Those kind of things you don't often see in an undergraduate, and they're not that clear. But I could see those in Jim."

Garhart specialized in narrative art — art that told a story. His drawing and printmaking classes helped Jim sharpen his skills. The most important lesson, though, came in the professor's office, near the end of Jim's sophomore year.

The deadline to choose a major was approaching. Jim knew he could draw, and do it quite well. But he was exasperated. His doubts were on a much deeper level. He wondered: How do you say anything with art?

Details of their conversation have faded with time, but the impact has not.

"We get students every now and then, and to even say that you're teaching them is, I think, a misnomer," Garhart says. "You just have to help them find their way. It's directing, it's not dictating at all. It's helping them understand their abilities."

Jim knew he could communicate by writing; that's why he'd come to Kenyon. After talking with Garhart, he understood better his ability to communicate using a visual language.

Jim's next project was a print called "Balloon Man." It was based on a fellow who sold balloons outside Cincinnati's old Crosley Field.

"Attached to it were a lot of my nostalgic feelings about my dad and going to ballgames with him," he says. "That was when (my work) started to change. I started to 'get it.' The work became a lot more personal, about my own life. Suddenly I'd turned the corner. There was no looking back after that."

As always, Jim returned home that summer and worked at the truck-painting shop. He also devoted time — 180 hours, to be exact — to the 1974 Banner Day competition sponsored by the Reds.

Jim and his girlfriend created a banner featuring facial drawings of Pete Rose, Johnny Bench, Joe Morgan and other Reds, with the theme "Ours in October." It won second place out of about 1,000 entries.

But it was the previous year's Banner Day, July 1, 1973, that he recalls most fondly. The Reds faced the Los Angeles Dodgers in a doubleheader.

With the first game still in progress, Jim, his girlfriend and other banner makers gathered at a designated spot in the bowels of what was then called Riverfront Stadium.

"You get down there, you can't hear anything but distant roars," Jim says. "We didn't know what was happening, we were just excited about our banner. We were first in line, and waiting, waiting, waiting."

Finally, with the game over, the door in the center-field wall opened.

"We walk in, and people are on their feet, roaring," Jim says. "We're walking around and the people are just going *nuts*. We're thinking, wow, this is *some* banner."

Turns out fans had just been treated to one the most memorable moments in Reds history: With two outs in the bottom of the ninth inning, reserve catcher Hal King hit a three-run homer to beat the Dodgers, 4-3.

That fall, Jim returned to Kenyon for his junior year. He was majoring in art, but was unsure where it would lead him.

"Really it never occurred to me that people made a living doing cartooning," he says. "I wasn't aimed at that. I thought I'd be a painter in a garret somewhere."

He and his roommate, Elder grad Jim Kraft, spent their weekends studying, watching

movies shown by the campus film society, and writing their girlfriends back home.

"We were not partyers, and we did not belong to fraternities," says Kraft, who now lives in Carmel, Ind. "Because we knew each other real well, I think if either of us had tried to do anything radical, the other might have said: 'What are you doing? You're not like that.'"

Chris Myers shared a campus art studio with Jim.

"He was one of those guys who never came out of his room when he was a freshman," says Myers, who now lives in Norton, Mass. "He studied all the time.

"I take credit for getting him out a little bit. I was a guitar player in a rock 'n' roll band, junior year. And since we were friends, Jim kept coming out to hear my band play. I just remember how out of character it was when he first started showing up.

"When he would come to the parties, he'd get out there and dance," Myers says. "This is the truth, and it has to be printed: He's one of the worst dancers on the planet. He's hilarious. The best way to describe Jim's dancing: He was part Jerry Lewis, part Tasmanian devil, and

The April 1975 Kenyon College *Bulletin* published Jim's serious drawings of famous Kenyon alumni, including, top, Henry Winter Davis, and, bottom, President Rutherford B. Hayes. Far right is the fall 1982 cover of the *Kenyon College Alumni Bulletin* which he created six years after joining *The Enquirer.*

maybe part Bill Laimbeer. Remember Bill Laimbeer? (A professional basketball player.) All elbows and knees, just spastic. It was like electroshock therapy."

Then it was back to the books.

"I never remember him complaining about schoolwork or pulling all-nighters," says Rich West, who was a political science major and now lives in Northampton, Mass. "He came to Kenyon with a work ethic. My impression always was he got that from his dad, from his family. He took school seriously and he excelled."

And yet, West says, "he had no real idea how he was going to use any of his talents and make a living. He often made the joke that about the only thing he would be qualified for would be a lumberjack."

During Jim's junior year, West became managing editor of the campus newspaper, the *Kenyon Collegian.* He wrote a series of stories on famous Kenyon alumni, and Jim agreed to do the

accompanying caricatures.

The drawings caught the eye of Joe Slate, a Kenyon art professor who had worked briefly for the *Seattle Times.* Slate took Jim under his wing. He told him about the demands of working for a daily newspaper, and encouraged him to do more work for the *Collegian.*

Jim, in fact, was already keenly interested in the work of Pat Oliphant and Jeff MacNelly, who were revolutionizing political cartooning. Until then, the craft had consisted largely of charcoal drawings with labels and heavy symbolism.

"These guys were drawing very sarcastic, satirical, sharp-edged cartoons," Jim says, "and they were really fun. So I was wandering along at precisely the right moment. Their drawings just started getting me. I wanted to know what this was all about."

Problem was, he didn't have a clue about how the political world worked. "It was never a love of politics that lit my fire," he says. "It was always a love of the drawing."

So Jim began immersing himself in current events.

His first editorial cartoon was supposed to illustrate an article on dissatisfaction at Kenyon. When the story was scrapped at the last minute, Jim's illustration ran alone in the last edition of

Fall 1982

Kenyon
College Alumni Bulletin

the *Collegian,* his junior year.

That summer of 1975, he wrote to MacNelly, who was working at the *Richmond* (Va.) *News Leader.* It was, Jim says, "the usual plaintive request for any tips he could give me. He didn't give me tips, but he sent a handwritten note. It was all the encouragement I needed. A thing like that puts wind in my sails for a long time."

When he returned to campus as a senior in the fall, he committed to drawing one editorial cartoon a week. It was the start of a pivotal year for Jim Borgman.

Then, as now, he rarely settled for simple images. And so in his dorm room, using a piece of Masonite propped against a card table as a drawing table, he typically worked long into the night, sometimes spending 10 hours on a political cartoon. (In contrast, today a complicated one might require two hours.)

"When you're learning your craft, every word, every line requires a major decision," he says. "Nothing just flows. Plus I was pretty consciously adopting a new art form. I always liked caricatures, but putting them into a real scene that's supposed to narrate a point, that was new."

One of his first efforts was "Gangster Cats."

"During the summer, a cat had run loose on campus. Students

"We were not partyers, and we did not belong to fraternities. Because we knew each other real well, I think if either of us had tried to do anything radical, the other might have said: 'What are you doing? You're not like that.'"

Jim Kraft

were not allowed to have pets, and (campus) security shot this cat. We all came back outraged, of course. And so I did a cartoon of a bunch of cats,

MY 25 FAVORITE CDS TO WORK TO

Over The Rhine / *Good Dog Bad Dog*
Sheryl Crow / *Sheryl Crow*
The Band / *Music from Big Pink*
Bob Dylan / *Blood on the Tracks*
Bruce Springsteen / *Ghost of Tom Joad*
Barenaked Ladies / *Stunt*
Vivaldi / *Four Seasons*
Paul Simon / *Graceland*
Ry Cooder / *Boomer's Story*
Mary Black / *No Frontiers*
David Arkenstone / *Standing Stones of Callanish*
Los Lobos / *Just Another Band from East L.A.*
Bruce Springsteen / *Born to Run*
Over The Rhine / *Till We Have Faces*
Rev. Gary Davis / *Harlem Street Singer*
Van Morrison/*Tupelo Honey*
Jimmy Cliff / *The Harder They Come*
Leo Kottke / *My Feet Are Smiling*
Henryk Gorecki / *Symphony No. 3*
Go-Go's / *God Bless the Go-Go's*
Natalie Merchant /*Tigerlily*
Paul Winter Consort / *Icarus*
B. B. King / *Deuces Wild*
Bruce Springsteen / *Nebraska*
O Brother, Where Art Thou? soundtrack

holed up in a room with tommy guns, like gangsters, peering out through the shades, making some comment about security having them cornered."

Many of his cartoons showcased his newfound interest in national politics. Meanwhile, he maintained his high academic standards. And as always, he doodled in class.

"He sat right in front of me, so I couldn't stop myself from watching him," says retired religion professor Donald Rogan, who was amused to see his face appear in Jim's notebook.

Rogan taught a class called "Jesus and the Gospels." Jim took it as an elective his senior year. Also in the class of about 40 was a religion honors student, Lynn Goodwin.

"I've joked that by the end of the semester, they were listening to each other more than they were listening to me," says Rogan. "It was obvious after a few weeks that they were becoming more than just friends."

Says Jim: "I borrowed her notes when I was away one weekend and missed a class. I returned them and brought her one of the prints I had made, as a thank you. It was a little too big of a gift to just be thanking her for her notes."

Which, of course, is exactly what he intended when he presented her with "Balloon Man."

By the middle of Jim's senior year, Rich West was prodding

him to send a portfolio of his *Collegian* editorial cartoons to his hometown newspaper, *The Cincinnati Enquirer*. The job offer that resulted was big news at Kenyon.

"He was the envy of campus because he landed not only a job," Myers says, "but what was perceived as a fairly cool gig. No one had ever heard of such a thing, getting hired before you'd even graduated. So we decided to throw a party for him."

In fact, there was much to celebrate about senior year. In Lynn Goodwin, Jim had found the woman he would marry. (Professor Rogan, an Episcopal priest, performed the ceremony a year later.) Jim had found how to say meaningful things with his art. He'd found a great job.

To top it off, he was awarded the Anderson Cup, a prestigious honor presented each year to the Kenyon student who has made significant contributions to the campus community.

Leaving wasn't easy.

"It ended up being the right place for me," Jim says. "I was nestled in there, and I loved it. I was in a community of open-minded people who loved intellectual debate. An editorial cartoonist could thrive in a place like that."

Now he had to prove himself on a bigger stage.

A Salute From A Colleague

Several of Jim's professional colleagues were asked to commemorate his silver anniversary at The Enquirer. *This drawing was created by Jim Davis, the creator of the comic strip* Garfield.

Chapter 4

PHILOSOPHY OF KINDNESS HELPS LAND ENQUIRER JOB

BY THOM GEPHARDT

Thom Gephardt joined the Enquirer in 1960 as editor of the editorial page and he continued in that job until he retired in 1992.

A major American newspaper hires an editorial cartoonist about as infrequently as the president of the United States hires a chief justice. And the process can be just as painstaking.

One reason for the rarity is that there are now fewer than 1,500 daily newspapers in the United States. Only about one in 10 has its own editorial cartoonist. The other nine find it more economical to buy cartoons from a newspaper syndicate at a fraction of the cost of maintaining a full-time staff cartoonist.

When L.D. Warren retired in 1974 after more than three decades as *The Cincinnati Enquirer's* cartoonist, there was no one in a decision-making position who had had any experience hiring a cartoonist. So where should we start? Was there a formula to guide us?

First of all, we concluded, we wanted someone with technical competence, someone who could draw attractive, inviting cartoons. Second, we wanted someone who had a solid grasp of the complex issues with which the community, the nation and the world were wrestling. Third, we wanted a cartoonist capable of producing not just an occasional good cartoon, but five or six cartoons a week, 52 weeks a year, year after year. Finally, our goal was a cartoonist who generally shared the convictions and principles for which the newspaper sought to stand. That's where the *Enquirer* stood when the name of James Mark Borgman arose.

It arose because Jim had had a chance meeting with Graydon DeCamp, an *Enquirer* editor, and with whom he shared his aspiration to become a cartoonist. That meeting encouraged Jim to call for an appointment. Then he appeared. He brought with him some of the cartoons he had drawn for the Kenyon College newspaper. He brought also an abundance of facial hair in the form of luxuriant sideburns, which proved to be a modest harbinger of what was to come.

As matters turned out, Jim was

an open, affable, congenial young man, confident but modest. After five minutes it was not difficult imagining him as a part of the *Enquirer* family, in some capacity. But when his credentials as an editorial cartoonist were laid alongside the *Enquirer's* arbitrary standards, he fell notably short.

Drawing a cartoon (even a clever, attractive cartoon) for a weekly student newspaper is a far cry from drawing a daily cartoon for a metropolitan daily. Jim, moreover, was no more engrossed in the march of political and economic events around the world than any other Midwestern college student. As for philosophy, he seemed to have none except, perhaps, for kindness.

So what made him a reasonable candidate, even an ideal candidate? The answer was enthusiasm, eagerness and an abundance of innocence. These are extraordinary qualities for anyone aspiring to a place in the ultracyncical world of journalism. When, as an illustration, he was shown the office recently vacated by L.D. Warren, he looked around and declared, "Gee whiz!" And when later the same day he filled out a formal application for employment and came to the question, "Starting salary expected," he wrote, "Whatever the job pays."

So Jim Borgman was not only acceptable, but inevitable. He got the job and went to work. He invested much of his time acquainting himself with the issues about which any cartoonist draws, and, as if by osmosis, he became comfortable and competent in any discussion of public affairs. He participated productively in the editorial page department's daily conferences, which determined what local, national and global issues deserved treatment.

He was also part of the process whenever notables came to visit the *Enquirer's* editorial board — Cabinet members, members of Congress, governors, presidential candidates. He listened and asked questions and he sketched. In the process he built up a voluminous collection of national newsmakers in their most relaxed moments — a collection that invariably wound up in editorial cartoons weeks, months or even years later.

He quickly devised a daily routine that rarely varied. It began after he had an opportunity to survey the day's news. From that survey came as many as five or six rough pencil sketches — embryonic cartoons. These he brought in for discussion. After a general agreement on the best idea for the day, Jim produced his finished cartoon, which was then on its way.

Jim never became so absorbed in these weighty public issues that he overlooked the human subjects about which Cincinnatians talked. And he learned quickly about the impact a cartoon can have. During a grim season for the Bengals, as an illustration, he drew a cartoon of Riverfront Stadium showing the scoreboard with the startling news: Bengals 3, Little Sisters of the Poor, 77. Before the day was out, a small delegation of members of that religious order filed into his office, utterly bewildered that the Little Sisters should be injected into a football cartoon. Once Jim had explained, they seemed pleased at the public notice.

I have a vivid memory of the announcement that the international financier Armand Hammer was lending a portion of his incredibly expensive art collection for a showing at the Cincinnati Art Museum. Jim's reaction was a cartoon depicting a museum filled with portraits of boxes of Arm & Hammer baking soda. One local art patron called completely aghast. Mr. Hammer, she figured, would be irreparably insulted; Cincinnati would never again see the Armand Hammer collection. As it turned out, Mr. Hammer was charmed when he eventually saw the cartoon and asked Jim for the autographed original.

"He brought with him some of the cartoons he had drawn for the Kenyon College newspaper. He brought also an abundance of facial hair in the form of luxuriant sideburns, which proved to be a modest harbinger of what was to come."

Thom Gephardt

"Quite apart from what he has done for the Enquirer *for a quarter of a century, no one can possibly catalog the hours Jim has contributed to making Cincinnati a better, more compassionate community."*

Thom Gephardt

I remember an occasion in the fall of 1981 when I was one of 18 editorial page editors from around the country who were invited to breakfast with President Reagan in the White House's Cabinet Room. The president, only eight months in office, burst into the room cheerfully waving a cartoon — a Jim Borgman cartoon. It showed one of the nation's liberal television commentators rendering his verdict on the Reagan economic program. He's saying (and President Reagan gleefully read): "And so it seems clear to this reporter that Reaganomics has failed . . . failed to thrive in a climate of optimism . . . failed to blossom into a viable economic alternative . . . failed to bear the fruit of prosperity — at least in these first five disappointing minutes." If having your work hailed by the president of the United States isn't fame, what is?

Quite apart from what he has done for the *Enquirer* for a quarter of a century, no one can possibly catalog the hours Jim has contributed to making Cincinnati a better, more compassionate community. He is besieged by requests that he produce a cartoon for one cause or another. He has requests for originals of particularly successful cartoons. He has spoken to groups large and small. Very

MY 25 FAVORITE PEOPLE TO DRAW

Bill Clinton
Marge Schott
Schottzie
Dan Quayle
Ronald Reagan
Simon Leis
David Mann
Richard Nixon
Jimmy Carter
Bob Bedinghaus
Mike Brown
Mike DeWine
Newt Gingrich
Jerry Springer
George W. Bush
Hillary Clinton
Ken Blackwell
Saddam Hussein
Steve Forbes
Bobbie Sterne
Pete Rose
Ross Perot
Yasser Arafat
Prince Charles
Jim Tarbell

nearly every cause that seeks his assistance receives it — and benefits from it. No one can catalog the pleasure he has brought to everyone who knows him — his simplicity, his generosity, his empathy — the qualities that endeared him to the *Enquirer* on the day of that first interview are robust and well.

It will always be a joy to me

that my life and my family's were often intertwined with his. His wedding in Kenyon's lovely Gothic chapel and the graciousness that allowed our 7-year-old daughter to imagine herself a member of the wedding party. The birth and growth of his gifted children. The high honors that came in recognition of his personal and professional achievements. The gestures of admiration and appreciation of those who were daily beneficiaries of his talent — gestures that were vicariously shared by all those who worked with him.

There were, of course, poignant and tearful moments as well — the death of his uncle, the Rev. Eugene Maly, one of the Catholic Church's biblical scholars of worldwide reputation; of his father, Big Jim Borgman, who set for Jim an example of loving service to friends and neighbors; and, of course, of his wife, Lynn, whose exceptional talents enhanced his career and his family's happiness.

Twenty-five years of memories. What a privilege to have stood in the shadows and watched the blossoming of a career built on talent, energy, consideration and, most of all, character. So what's there to say in looking back over such a quarter century? Only one thing comes to mind: Gee whiz!

A Salute From A Colleague

Several of Jim's professional colleagues were asked to commemorate his silver anniversary at The Enquirer. *This drawing was created by Lynn Johnston, creator of the comic strip* For Better or For Worse.

February 21, 1985
I can always count on a pothole cartoon during the spring thaw.

"UM... EXCUSE US WHILE WE GO POWDER OUR NOSES."

November 6, 1987
Bobbie Sterne's election to Cincinnati City Council in 1987 ended an all-male streak in city representation
as well as adding another great face to a highly caricaturable council.

"THERE'S THE OLD CINCINNATI 'CAN'T DO' SPIRIT!"

January 10, 1988
Incapable of finding productive work, City Council busied itself with bans
on yard sales, pit bulls, tailgate parties and other trivialities.

September 16, 1990
I've never voted against a school levy, but sometimes it's really hard to cast that vote.

April 18, 2001
When Timothy Thomas was killed running from the police, it seemed we would finally address some underlying racial attitudes in Cincinnati. Weak leadership, though, foils the best of intentions.

"I TOLD YOU THIS WOULD HAPPEN....DO WE HAVE A RIBBON HE CAN CUT?"

May 26, 1981
David Mann was a cartoonist's dream. His ribbon-cuttings seemed to symbolize
the absence of real mayoral power in Cincinnati.

"THAT'S A FIRST!... JUST AS I WAS USHERING THEM IN, THEY UP AND SCALED THE FENCE."

January 2, 1998
Maurice McCrackin and Ernest Bromley protested for peace before, during and after it was fashionable.
At age 85 Mac was arrested for trying to scale the White House fence, an inspiration to us aging rabble rousers.

August 22, 1986
We continued to tolerate our dysfunctional city government because
every proposed alternative was incomprehensible.

January 17, 1999
Why can't Ohio elect a cartoon governor like Jesse Ventura?

July 21, 1994
I drew the Jimmy Carter White House as a barrel of monkeys in 1978,
but I could draw (and observe) better monkeys by 1994.

"TESTING...TESTING....THERE ONCE WAS A GIRL FROM NANTUCKET..."

August 24, 1984
President Reagan appeared on Fountain Square just days after an infamous episode in which he joked
unknowingly into an open microphone about bombing Russia. I drew another cartoon in which President Reagan,
the stand-up comedian, stood before a mushroom cloud saying, "I've got a million of 'em."

"GOOD NEWS, GOVERNOR! I'VE FOUND A BUYER FOR HOME STATE..... AND HE'S GIVING US A HECK OF A DEAL!"

March 19, 1985
Ticket scalper Bill Meister was arguably one shade more ethical
than Home State leader Marvin Warner.

DEADLINE MONSTER OFTEN CREATES HIS FAVORITE CARTOON

BY JIM BORGMAN

When Jim Borgman joined the Enquirer and heard editors hollering "Copy!" to summon clerks, he thought they were ordering "coffee." During his first weeks in the newspaper business he unsuccessfully tried to screw up the courage to yell, "Cream and sugar!"

"Of all the cartoons you have drawn, what's your favorite?"

It's the question that always stumps me.

In a profession where the Deadline Monster eats cartoons like they're popcorn at a scary movie, my favorite cartoon is the one that, God willing, I'll think of in the next hour before the Monster shakes me down again.

My favorites aren't always your favorites. I'll hang a cartoon on my studio bulletin board if I finally got the bags under Clinton's eyes right or if I managed to squeeze a record ninth cigarette into Marge's mouth. I may like the expression I caught on a minor character's face in the background or a play on words that pleased me in the caption. The cartoon might otherwise underwhelm as a whole, but I think of it fondly whenever I happen upon it later.

Sometimes one of your favorites becomes one of my favorites because I can see how much you liked it. The giant tiger commanding the football field when the Bengals got off to a big start one year began showing up on banners at the stadium as much as John 3:16. Kids were sending me their crayoned versions and radio stations passed out T-shirts.

Truth be told, I'm not a big football fan, but it was fun to see you snatch that one up.

Likewise, there may be something special about the experience of drawing it that makes a cartoon a favorite. When Ryan White, the young AIDS victim whose classmates had been afraid to come near him, finally died, I drew a pencil sketch of him being embraced in heaven. Below I wrote: "A place where no one is afraid to hug."

I saw the drawing on my paper before I was aware of thinking the thought. It moved me to tears, as though someone else had drawn it and placed it in front of me. I had the distinct experience of having been used

Jim says he is often surprised by the reader's choice of favorites. General Norman Schwarzkopf said this was his favorite cartoon and it was a favorite of the jury which selected drawings for this book. Jim did not pick it as one of his 25 favorites.

Again, thank you for my favorite editorial cartoon, and taking the time to write such a supportive letter.

Sincerely,

H. NORMAN SCHWARZKOPF

to get an idea into the world. That will always be one of my favorites.

Farewell cartoons when a prominent person dies are often favorites of readers. Big Klu. Cardinal Bernardin. Mother Teresa evoked a lot of positive response from readers. The drawing seems to provide a cathartic moment for the community, a sort of secular requiem, a moment when we all focus on one life story before moving on.

My own favorite was of Richard Nixon in that pivotal moment before God sorts out the record.

There's also something bonding about a shared experience, like the cicada invasions, that tends to yield up favorites. These sex-crazed bugs live in the ground for almost two decades, only to emerge for a week or two of wild insect orgies. Two cicadas sitting in a bar: "It's down to this, Artie — Seventeen years wasted if we don't get lucky tonight."

But what makes my own antennae tingle?

I love doing a cartoon that requires no words to get its point across. Those are tough to pull off. I was able to draw Gorbachev as the last domino

MY 25 FAVORITE SOURCES FOR CARTOON IDEAS

National Public Radio / *Morning Edition*
The Onion
New York Times Op-Ed Page
Starbucks Grande Latte
Enquirer reporters
Brookstone catalogue
Nightline
CityBeat
My family
Jerry Scott
Daniel Schorr commentaries
Daydreaming
Anna Quindlen columns
Children's section of the library
NPR / *All Things Considered*
Fresh Air / Terri Gross
Charlie Rose
Reds on Radio
Prairie Home Companion
New Yorker
Car Talk
Bruegger's Bagels
Long car trips
Washington Post Weekly Review
The shower

about to fall as the Soviet Union collapsed. When the teacher Christa McAuliffe died aboard the space shuttle Challenger, a child's hand holding an apple up to the stars was all I could say. And as Kenneth Starr rolled out the lurid details of the Monica Lewinsky business, I drew the Lincoln Memorial with

a shocked Abe holding his ears. No words. That's using the visual power of the medium, not just tacking a picture onto a punch line.

And I suppose that comes closest to the heart of what makes a cartoon a favorite of mine. Editorial cartooning is a sophisticated weapon — a laser, capable of splitting the hair on a politician's head. Good cartoons can make us wince, gasp, laugh, turn purple, ponder, retort or snort coffee out our noses. The best cartoons make us do several of these at once. Words and pictures dovetail. Layers unfold. Subtleties emerge.

It saddens me when my profession is dumbed down, like it has been in recent years, when cartoonists use it like a butter knife instead of a rapier. National news magazines print only the least-common-denominator cartoons, the ones you'd understand if you did nothing but glance at the headlines a few times a week. Bam. One quick joke and you're out. It's the Jay Leno-izing of a once-powerful art form, and its practitioners are rewarded with

"I love doing a cartoon that requires no words to get its point across. Those are tough to pull off. I was able to draw Gorbachev as the last domino about to fall as the Soviet Union collapsed."

Jim Borgman

reprints from sea to shining sea.

That kind of cartooning reminds me of those sad-looking bears that wear silly hats and pedal bikes in the circuses. Editorial cartoonists have forgotten the power they have in the wild, the ferocity of Thomas Nast's attacks on the corrupt Boss Tweed, the outrage of Herblock and Paul Conrad during the Vietnam War, the courage of Bill Mauldin standing up to Jim Crow, the venom in Pat Oliphant's portraits of Nixon when he put himself above the law.

Walt Kelly, the creator of *Pogo*, spent some years as an editorial cartoonist. He compared editorial cartoonists to watchdogs, barking at every sound in the night. More often than not, the rustling in the yard is a harmless squirrel or a newspaper blown across the grass. But when it's a burglar, you'll be glad we raised a ruckus.

So what makes me mad? Spoiled ballplayers. Deceptive presidents. Half-baked medical bulletins. Ignorant racists. Spoilers of the environment. Hypocritical holy men. Gas price manipulation. Stadiums over schools. Gun nuts. Acceptance of mediocrity. Pedophile priests. People who'd rather fight for blastocysts than the homeless folks they step over on the street.

Child pornographers. Stupid people in high places. Mammoth SUVs. The fact that my street never gets plowed.

I grew up in this baseball town, so I compare editorial cartooning to pitching. If I tried to throw fastballs every day, readers would soon adjust their timing and start lining my arguments right back up the middle. No, the secret to pitching (and daily cartooning) is to change speeds. Sunday might be a fastball about blacks and cops, Monday a slow curve on the topic of Internet addiction. Wednesday might be a slider about funding schools, followed by a blooper pitch about the Bengals' latest bruising. If I'm doing my job, readers should never know what's coming. Which is what makes it fun.

In recent years, some of my favorite cartoons have been scenes from our households, regular doughy Midwestern folks dealing with changes in technology and the ever-faster pace of life. I absolutely love drawing these snapshots from daily life: the moment the woman realizes her toaster oven is also a fax machine; that the guy's large body has been subdivided into three area codes; that working 24/7 is no longer enough — now it's 25/7.

In the course of my 25 years of cartooning, the news has changed from a Washington-centric study in House bills and housing policies to a fractured patchwork of concerns about social causes, health research and lifestyle issues closer to home. Whereas I used to caricature the Speaker of the House and assume readers would know who he was, I daresay I may never have even drawn Dennis Hastert in his several years at the helm (and had to look up the spelling of his name when I wrote this.)

It's not that people stopped caring about government. It's just that times are good enough for most people that we momentarily have the luxury of focusing on the compelling adventure of our own lives and the way the world is changing them. That's what the Founding Fathers hoped would happen. It's a good thing. When there is no single national story line I can assume we're all following, so the news can look like a pebbled and trivial landscape. Shark bites and tire recalls. A break in the action. Shrug.

But as long as my voice holds out, I'll be the blasted watchdog barking at the sounds in the night. Somebody has to raise hell if the sounds get too close. There are still burglars out there, tyrants, bullies, madmen, bad guys. And they aren't going to be caught by bicycling bears.

"Good cartoons can make us wince, gasp, laugh, turn purple, ponder, retort or snort coffee out our noses. The best cartoons make us do several of these at once."

Jim Borgman

May 5, 1987
Drawn in the early days of the growing AIDS crisis, the visual here made the whole point.

March 31, 1996
I have a tortured relationship with baseball and needed a prop to express my feelings.
The talking baseball invariably betrays my optimism much as Lucy's football betrays Charlie Brown.

THE BILL COMES DUE

November 2, 1992
On a lucky day, everything works. I felt I made a thoughtful observation, nailed the caricatures
and hit a funny bone. Bush's lanky body still makes me laugh.

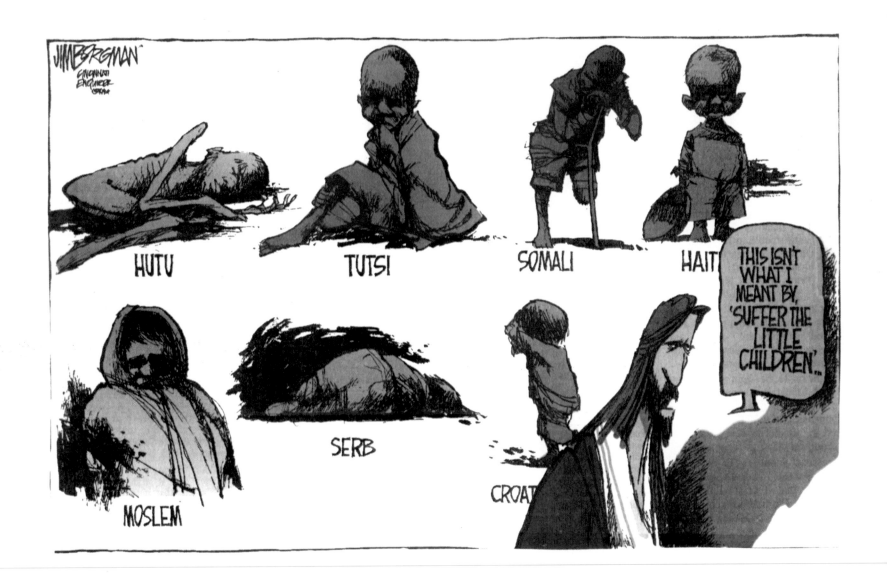

July 31, 1994
I hesitate to feature Jesus too often in my work, but sometimes his words say it all.

June 4, 1987
Nothing brings us together like the 17-year cicada invasions.
Theirs is a display of raw procreation that even Simon Leis can't stop.

December 17, 1995
You have to laugh at the way our town panics at the first forecast of snow.
The TV weather alarmists should be charged with inciting mass hysteria.

May 4, 1990
A friend who lived near Fernald once had me over for a swim in a swimming hole on
his property . . . which I came to regret as the reports of ground contamination mounted.

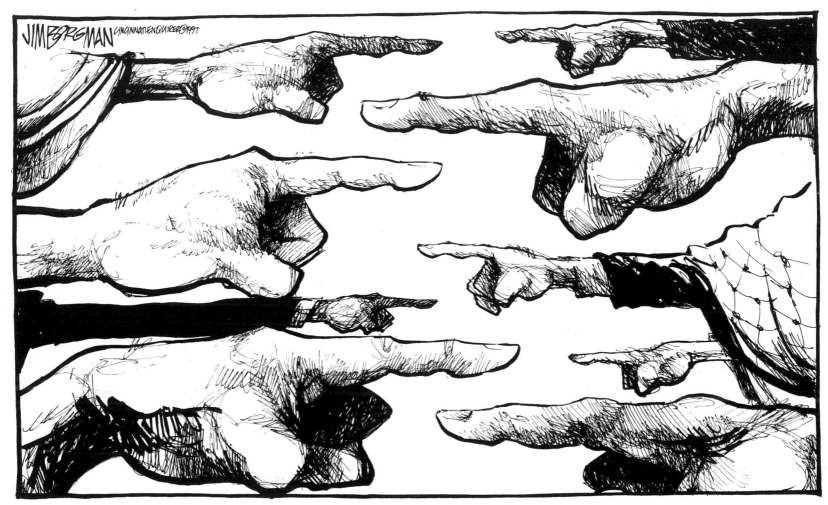

A BRIEF HISTORY OF MIDEAST RELATIONS

November 19, 1997
I have little more to say about the cycle of violence in the Middle East.
This drawing could rerun every week.

January 31, 1999
President Clinton met with the Pope on his visit to the United States during
the height of the president's scandal-ridden second term.

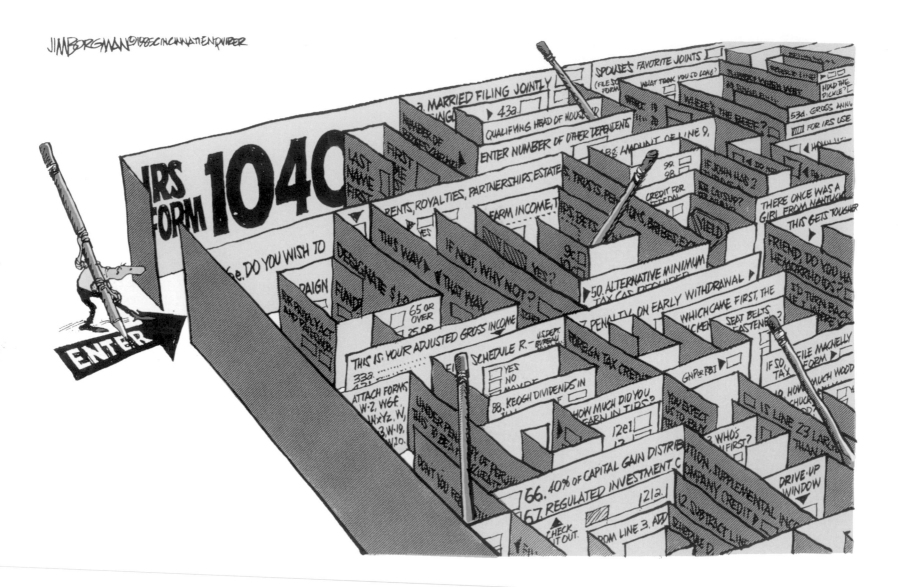

February 12, 1985
Tax forms, and other left-brain exercises, appear impenetrable to me. I don't mind paying the taxes
as much as I mind the search for the amount the government thinks I should pay.

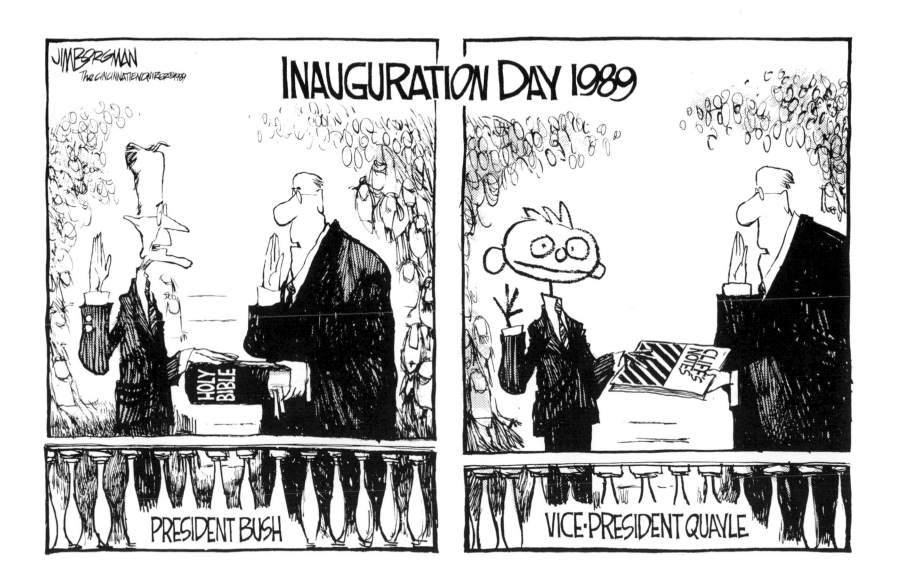

January 12, 1989
Dan Quayle was hard to caricature in a conventional way. It was only when I scrawled a stick figure with a crayon
in my left hand that I captured the childlike, half-baked, intellectual lightweight we have all come to know.

"I STILL DON'T SEE WHAT'S SO OFFENSIVE ABOUT THESE CHARACTERS, DO YOU, BOOGERFLICKER?"

March 5, 1992
Kenner launched a line of toys with what I considered gross names and the company seemed
startled by the public disgust. I tried to outdo the company's lack of taste.

JIMBORGMAN CINCINNATI ENQUIRER©1988

BIG KLU
1924-1988

April 1, 1988
Ted Kluszewski's playing days were just before my time, but I remember my dad telling me how
Klu had ripped the sleeves off his jersey to free his biceps.

September 13, 1998
Kenneth Starr was the only person who seemed to relish his lurid report on President Clinton's raunchy
involvement with Monica Lewinsky. Most of us were mortified.

May 12, 1996
When Cincinnatians travel, we invariably encounter people familiar with and critical of Marge Schott's gaffes.

December 2, 1992

I cut no slack for racism. With her epithet about her "million-dollar nigger," Marge Scott turned from a lovable buffoon into an embarrassing lout. I take it as a personal insult that she represents our city to so many people.

Meet Jennifer.

She's just fourteen.

Too young to be taught about the facts of life.
Too sweet to be troubled with the confusion of sex.
Too innocent to have her happy world disturbed.

Meet Jennifer's daughter.

May 3, 1985
Teachers tell me this is a favorite with them and I have seen it on a lot of school bulletin boards.

NEXT....

October 6, 1988
Remember when the Bengals were steamrolling over every opponent in the Super Bowl season of '88?
This image started showing up as an unofficial symbol of the season.

"CANCEL MY APPOINTMENTS ..... THIS ONE MAY TAKE AWHILE."

April 23, 1994
It's considered bad form to slam a dead person. But sugarcoating President Nixon's life was implausible.
This cartoon pleased me because I was able to put the mess in God's hands.

July 20, 1990
There was no joy for me in chronicling Pete Rose's headfirst dive into infamy.
My brother and I still have a ball he autographed for us during his rookie season.

June 25, 1995
I probably should have said "thousands of years."

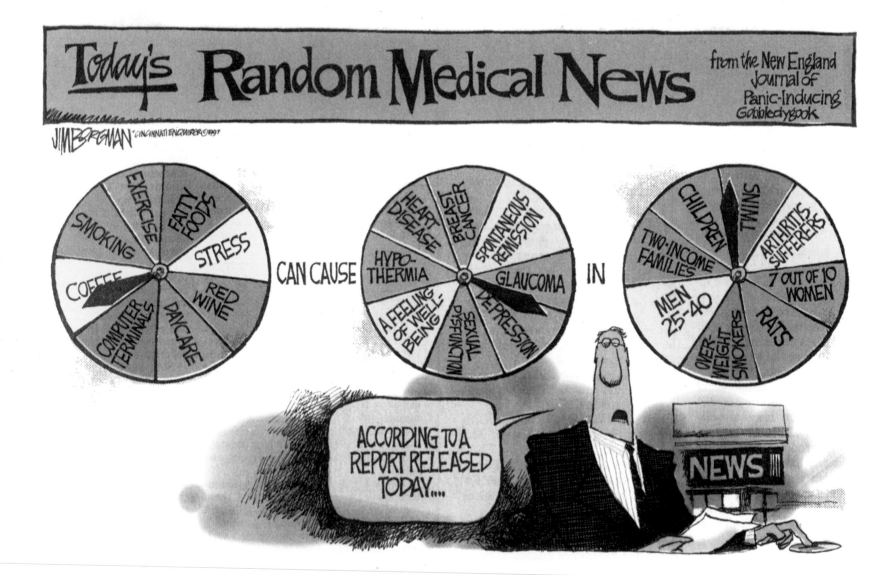

April 27, 1997
The health bulletins the press reports seem so arbitrary and undigested.
You can be sure that tomorrow's story will contradict yesterday's.

October 4, 1995
The obvious miscarriage of justice in the O.J. Simpson trial, which left
white America sputtering, was familiar turf for black America.

CHOOSE the REAL SEAT OF POWER in AMERICA

July 7, 1992
When you follow politics too closely, it's easy to forget where the real leverage lies.

"....ON THE BRIGHT SIDE, THE ENDANGERED SPECIES LIST IS DOWN TO ONE."

April 21, 1995
I don't know much about the science of rain forests, spotted owls or ozone depletion. But it's perfectly clear to me that every negative impact man has on Earth's environment has unintended consequences we live to regret.

Downtown Always A Favorite Hometown Target

By Allen Howard

Reporter and columnist Allen Howard joined the Enquirer ***in 1968. During his career at the newspaper he served with Jim on the*** Enquirer's ***editorial board for nine years.***

The sign in the cartoon reads "Cincinnati Grudgingly Invites You to View Elvis/Velvet."

The hallway shows a poster of Elvis Presley, with visitors to the Contemporary Arts Center viewing it. Underneath a cartoon couple going to the show, a line reads: "It's a challenging show — I don't know how they snuck it past the censors."

Satirical, funny and at the same time thought-provoking.

That is why Jim Borgman attacks the most serious issues in Greater Cincinnati. He makes you laugh. He makes you angry, and he picks a fight without trying.

The velvet Elvis cartoon was a snap at the controversy over the Robert Mapplethorpe show in April 1990.

Jim says he has little interest in Mapplethorpe or what he displays in his shows. While the city and prosecutors wrestled with the idea of censoring the show, Jim chose to make light of the controversy. That is how he views his job as an editorial cartoonist at the *Enquirer*.

"This was an issue that polarized the city. I am certainly not an advocate of Mapplethorpe art and I didn't particularly like the show, but I recognize the right of people to see whatever they want," he said.

He didn't pick a fight this time. With a little satire, he spread humor on a flaming controversy.

Sitting at his drawing board on the 19th floor of the *Enquirer* building, Jim has a panoramic view that stretches from his native Price Hill in the west, across the Ohio River and Northern Kentucky, to the foundation of the new baseball stadium in the east.

Each day, he can record the progress of urban development — or the lack of it. Sometimes he sees failed development plans on the Ohio side of the river while Northern Kentucky moves slightly ahead.

He captured that vision in a cartoon September 27, 1998, showing the Northern Kentucky skyline in the background with a "Welcome to Northern Kentucky" sign. On the Ohio side of the river, city and county officials look over plans near a bulldozer. The caption reads; "No, wait, Let's build the stadium six inches to the left."

This cartoon was a favorite of Chris Griffin, owner of the Spy Club, at Fifth and Plum streets downtown.

"This cartoon sets the tone for what we have been seeing for the last seven or eight years," Mr. Griffin said. "The city held me up for years before I was allowed to operate."

Much of what Jim sees aggravates him: a small business chased out of downtown by city officials, a $450 million football stadium that sits empty most of the year, a big hole in the ground where a department store was suppose to be.

Jim's cartoons attack and sometimes are perceived as insulting and condescending, but most of the time humor is the dominating element of his drawings.

His satire can be piercing, disturbing and often critical. But what the cartoons represent are pieces of Price Hill, West End, Over-the-Rhine, Avondale and other neighborhoods challenging the ineptness of big-city, downtown government through the eyes of an artist.

It is hard to classify Jim politically. A pragmatic liberal emerges when he takes a stand for gay rights, race, the environment and freedom of speech and expression.

And he reveals a streak of conservatism, when he paints a bridge between City Hall and the Hamilton County Courthouse, saying "The New Bridge Cincinnati Really Needs."

His favorite issues are local — politics, health, race, development, environment, parking, riots and stadiums — although he is quick to say his cartoons are not ideological. They are just Jim Borgman, urging his readers to get involved.

"I feel when I am dealing with local issues, I can have some impact," he said. "There is nothing more futile than me sitting here drawing about foreign affairs."

He found plenty of grist for his cartoons when he was hired by the *Enquirer* in 1976. He wasn't sure how his liberal inclinations would fit at a conservative newspaper.

He didn't know if he was supposed to be the devil's advocate or the burr under the saddle, but he had no problems blending his views with those of the newspaper's editorial page.

"I was pretty much given the green light to say what I wanted to say," he said. "Sometimes we agree, but I think it is coincidental when we do."

But some conservative readers took him to task.

"I think they felt they had to put me in my place," he said. "There were very vicious calls and letters. I learned to listen. One person called and started screaming. I let him talk, and finally he settled down."

Often, he said, readers completely miss the point of the cartoon, and he has to explain it. Then there are those who get an immediate chuckle.

Ken Million, a downtowner, is still laughing about the cartoon about the hole left by Nordstrom. It appeared December 1, 2000, after the city lost its bid to get Nordstrom to build a store downtown.

The cartoon showed a pit with a Klansman in the pit standing by a cross. The caption read "Problem Solved."

"He is usually right on the money," Mr. Million said. "He says what I want to say, but he is able to wrap it in humor. He makes you laugh at the issue, but the point is very well taken."

He doesn't want to be known as a person who picks fights, but he admits that's part of his profession.

"I received a letter and the person had ripped out a cartoon and marked it up," he said. "I didn't really like that because I am just trying to get a point

"This was an issue that polarized the city. I am certainly not an advocate of Mapplethorpe art and I didn't particularly like the show, but I recognize the right of people to see whatever they want."

Jim Borgman

across."

He has the ability to reach beyond common sense to present a contradictory issue and make it sound like the truth. A cartoon published April 19, 1987, shows a police officer writing a ticket to a person holding a balloon. The caption says, "Please, no fun outside Entertainment Zone."

Jim's eminent humor has been used artistically to paint a picture of Cincinnati and some of its most notorious personalities.

He produced a classic on the indelible Marge Schott, former Cincinnati Reds owner notorious for her foot-in-mouth statements.

The cartoon ran December 6, 1992. Schott embraces a caricature of Jesse Jackson, who stands next to the Rev. Al Sharpton, Spike Lee and a non-celebrity, all wearing caps marked with Malcolm's "X."

Schott tells Jackson, "I know how you feel, honey. . .. I'm a big Xavier fan myself."

Cincinnati attorney Robert Manley, who lives and works downtown, has Jim's cartoons on his office wall at 225 W. Court St.

His favorites include the Nordstrom hole and the bridge from City Hall to the Hamilton County Courthouse.

"To me they all show a total lack of confidence in city government," Manley said. "The Nordstrom hole shows the ineptitude of our city officials. And have you noticed that the parking lot that is there now is mostly empty?"

Jim may still ponder whether he is the devil's advocate or burr under the saddle, but, for sure, he has the knack to fire up the American debate.

While Jim denies that his cartoons relate to a political ideology, his liberalism is often vivid and pronounced. He is able to project it with a common man's touch, perhaps using much of the blue-collar background and the Price Hill working-class neighborhood where he grew up.

His cartoons that mirror his liberal philosophy can be considered a carricature of himself.

The late Jake Held once cracked after appearing before the *Enquirer* Editorial Board: "I was interviewed by an editorial writer and a cartoonist, wearing blue jeans."

Blue jeans and blue collar are part of Jim's common man persona and humor. You see that in a cartoon published on February 10, 1988, about the bus strike in Cincinnati. It shows two passengers at a bus stop on the west side. One is holding a Cheviot sign and the other is trying to hitchhike a ride. The caption reads: "You know, Alma, this bus strike is really beginning to frost my shorts."

His liberal tendencies have often caught him working against that grain and he enjoys that.

"I accept controversy as part of the job. Invariably when the crowd is going one way, I find myself going the other way," Jim said.

A February 24, 1981, cartoon shows a caricature of Simon Leis on Fountain Square screaming, "Let me tell you, my friends, we've got trouble! Right here in River City ! With a capital 'T' and that rhymes with 'P' and that stands for PORN!"

Then Jim can shift gears and manufacture a piece of dry humor with something as simple as the slow pace of snow removal in Kentucky, as shown in a cartoon that ran January 27, 1994. It shows a man, dressed in a heavy coat, scarf and snow cap, using an electric hairdryer to remove the snow. The caption reads, "Kentucky snow removal department begins to make headway."

Both cartoons give an example of the extent of his intellectual agility. In one moment, Jim can be aggressive, even to the point of antagonizing, but tempered with humor. Again he can rebound

"His favorite issues are local — politics, health, race, development, environment, parking, riots and stadiums — although he is quick to say his cartoons are not ideological. They are just Jim Borgman, urging his readers to get involved."

Allen Howard

3001 A.D.

HE WAS OBVIOUSLY SOMEONE VERY IMPORTANT TO EARLY CINCINNATITES...

CONGRATULATIONS, JIM!

A SALUTE FROM A COLLEAGUE

Several of Jim's professional colleagues were asked to commemorate his silver anniversary at The Enquirer. *This drawing was created by Mike Luckovich, Pulitzer Prize winning cartoonist of the Atlanta* Journal-Constitution.

with a simple, subtle approach to a touchy subject. He leaves the reader angry or laughing, but most of the time thinking seriously.

"He can bring you the thought you need on that morning when you don't want to do serious reading or serious thinking," said Million. "I live and work downtown. Over the years, I have become dismayed with the slow pace of development and watching much of what we had erode away. Just pick a Jim Borgman cartoon and see him cut through the maze and bring us right to what is going on in one caricature."

September 27, 1998
On the other hand, Kentucky development frequently seems
to go off without a hitch while Ohioans flap their gums.

A MALL AND the NIGHT VISITORS

December 12, 1993
My buddy Tom DeVoge thought of this idea so I snuck his name and hometown onto a shopping bag.
Naming mall stores is one of my favorite pastimes.

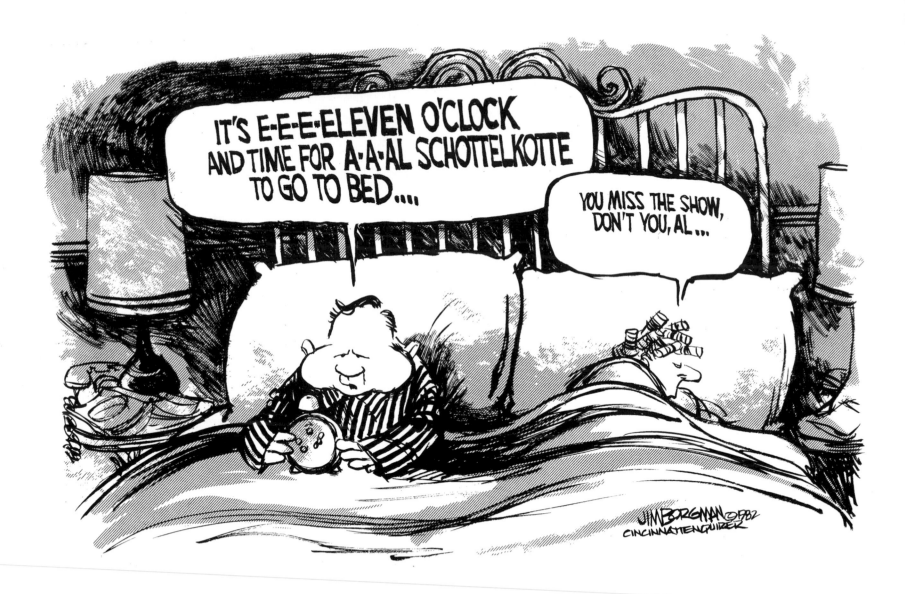

July 4, 1982
Before happy chatter, broadcasters such as Al Schottelkotte presented
just the facts — with all the flair of Joe Friday.

November 3, 1985
Architecture is tough to cartoon with all of its straight lines and right angles.
Give me a good expressive face any day.

February 24, 1981
There is still no funnier sight in Greater Cincinnati than the annual Simon Leis flotilla at the Harvest Home Festival.

" ...IT'S JUST AN OLD LEGEND, SON. THEY SAY THAT BACK BEFORE THE WINTER OF 1978 THERE WAS A CITY HERE."

January 31, 1978
Call me a communist, but big snows are fun.

CINCINNATI ESTABLISHES A DOWNTOWN 'ENTERTAINMENT DISTRICT'

April 19, 1987
Discussion of a downtown "entertainment zone" amuses me. Shouldn't it be
entertaining everywhere? And just who is defining "entertainment"?

KENTUCKY SNOW REMOVAL DEPT. BEGINS TO MAKE HEADWAY

January 27, 1994
When school closings were read on snowy days, my children would plead for us to move to Kentucky.

"YOU KNOW, ALMA, THIS BUS STRIKE IS REALLY BEGINNING TO FROST MY SHORTS..."

February 10, 1988

It's always fun to dip into my cast of doughy west-siders, first cousins of the people in my childhood neighborhood.
(When discussing east and west in Cincinnati, I can legitimately claim credentials in each region.)

January 19, 1990
This was the culmination of a weeklong series I drew on the "wall" that divides east from west in Cincinnati.
The division is a favorite joke we tell on ourselves. This story was told as a parody of the Berlin Wall's demise in Germany.

"IT'S A CHALLENGING SHOW — I DON'T KNOW HOW THEY SNUCK IT PAST THE CENSORS...."

April 16, 1990
After the Mapplethorpe brouhaha, I wondered if our arts institutions would be cowed
and if we were in for a siege of innocuous art.

May 2, 1999
Our steadiness and solidity as a region are a blessing and a curse. In a city that tends to constrict,
I see it as my role to light a fire, to insist on elbow room, to set off firecrackers under the principal's chair.

December 6, 1992
Marge Schott's infamous racial epithets brought a parade of African-American leaders to town for some sensitivity sessions.
At the same time, the emblem "X" from the movie *Malcolm X* was appearing on caps everywhere.

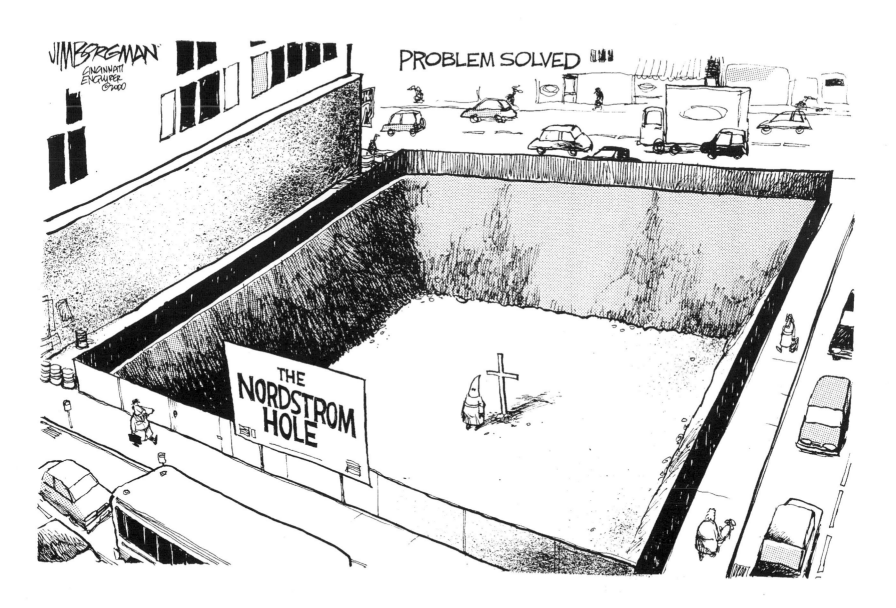

December 1, 2000
The annual dilemma — how to handle the issue of displaying the Klan cross — seemed easy
when another proposed downtown development project fell through.

Chapter 7

THE DAY THELMA SPIEGELMEIER SACKED A BENGAL QUARTERBACK

BY TIM SULLIVAN

Sports columnist Tim Sullivan joined The Enquirer six months after Jim Borgman was hired by the newspaper.

Whenever someone had the temerity to tell him a picture was worth a thousand words, the great sportswriter Red Smith had a ready reply.

"What picture?" he'd ask. "Whose words?"

Writers tend to look at the world more literally than artists, and we're petty enough to keep score. The Mona Lisa is surely magnificent, but for 996 words you could have Lincoln's Gettysburg Address (268), Hamlet's soliloquy (261), Cole Porter's "Begin The Beguine" (201), John Donne's "Death Be Not Proud" (123), the opening sentence of Charles Dickens' *A Tale Of Two Cities* (119) and the complete text of "The Purple Cow" (24). I point this out to provide hope for those of us perpetually playing keyboard catchup with Jim Borgman. Hope springs eternal. One of these centuries, the guy might go into a slump.

For nearly 25 years, I've been trying to arrange 1,000 words worthy of one Borgman cartoon, and there's no surer route to despair. Our career paths have run parallel — Jim's on the high road to the Pulitzer Prize; mine on the Bataan Death March that is the Cincinnati Bengals. If the *Enquirer*'s editorial cartoonist weren't such a frightfully fine fellow, I probably would have poisoned him by now.

Jim has the maddening ability to capture the essence of an event or an individual with the curl of a lip or the arch of an eyebrow. His caricatures are crafted as precisely as an Emerson essay, and his messages are similarly unmistakable and unerring.

His medium is not as confining as haiku or scrimshaw, but it requires the ability to express an opinion in a small space, in one dimension, and (most days) in black and white. Jim Borgman figures he gets five to 10 seconds of a reader's attention. His challenge is to get his point across in less time than most people afford telephone solicitors.

"This guy has a genius for

what he does," said Bengals owner Mike Brown, while reviewing some of Borgman's most skewering sketch work. "He just can send a real cutting message, and there's always some truth to it. It makes you laugh at the same time. That's a pretty unusual combination."

What's more unusual about Jim Borgman is that he is a newspaper superstar who engenders no jealousy. There is nothing collaborative about his editorial cartoons, yet his Pulitzer Prize was celebrated at the *Enquirer* as if every colleague shared in the credit. In my experience, the only other time an individual award spawned so much selfless joy was when Tony Perez was elected to the Baseball Hall of Fame.

Borgman and Perez have much in common — a lack of pretense, an abundance of decency, an ability to perform under pressure, an enduring affection for baseball. Jim has held on to all of his boyhood baseball cards and keeps an autographed Pete Rose ball among the artifacts in his home studio. There, on a typical summer night, he often works with the mellifluous background music of Reds broadcasts. When things aren't going well — say a Reds runner is stranded at third base — Jim Borgman has been

known to hurl his brushes.

You can take the boy out of Price Hill, but only so far.

"I'm not a sports cartoonist," he said. "I'm only drawing sports when it makes its way into the larger world of news. (But) I love it when we're in a good season and you can take off on the nuances.

"The Big Red Machine had fascinating characters — Perez, Rose, (Johnny) Bench with the big hammy hands and that Oklahoma sort of head, (Joe) Morgan as sharp and fast as he was. . .. A guy like Eric Davis would have been fun to draw day in and day out."

Bench owns several Borgman originals and says he's "proud to have them."

Cal Levy, the Reds marketing director, has three Borgmans hanging in his office at Cinergy Field, and three more at home.

"I can't draw a stick-figured cat," Levy said. "My family will tell you I refuse to play Pictionary. I admire any guy who can transfer what they've got in their head to what's on the page."

Among the cartoons that failed to make the cut for this volume — and it's reason enough for a sequel — was one Borgman drew of the young Eric Davis soaring above Riverfront Stadium to steal a home run. Like his later

drawing depicting Ken Griffey Jr.'s arrival in Cincinnati — the one captioned, "New monument unveiled on Fountain Square" — Borgman's Davis drawing nailed the mood of Reds fans contemplating a ballplayer of limitless possibilities.

More than that, both cartoons convey Jim's enduring sense of wonder about elite athletes. He is no longer the awestruck kid who secured Rose's signature at a Knights of Columbus father-son function, but neither has he become jaded as his innocence evaporates. Jim Borgman's cartoons can be cutting, but they are rarely cynical. Looking back, he laments missed opportunities to depict the charity work of some of his sports targets.

Mainly, he means Sam Wyche, the big-hearted Bengals coach with the wacky ways. But though their politics are at polar extremes, the cartoonist also yearns to draw a more flattering portrait of Marge Schott.

Of all Borgman's subjects, Schott comes closest to a human caricature. Brash and bigoted, craggy and chain-smoking, beloved by big dogs and small minds, the outrageous Reds owner was a recurring source of choice material. An informal competition developed between Borgman and sports cartoonist Jerry Dowling to see

"This guy has a genius for what he does. He just can send a real cutting message, and there's always some truth to it. It makes you laugh at the same time. That's a pretty unusual combination."

Mike Brown

who could squeeze more cigarettes in Schott's mouth.

"He was winning," Borgman admitted, "until I started sticking them in her ears."

Exaggeration, of course, is the essence of caricature. And athletes often make attractive models because of their outsized dimensions and musculature. Yet, when Borgman seizes on a subject, he generally focuses more on facial features than body types. Another of his masterpieces missing from this volume (and why wasn't I consulted on the selections?) is an eight-panel portrait projection of Pete Rose in exile. Each frame shows Rose a little older and angrier than the last, but all of them feature the same granite chin and two-strike glare.

(One quibble: The 1978 fantasy in which a star-struck Babe Ruth asks Rose for his autograph makes the Bambino look as if he's auditioning for the role of Quasimodo in *The Hunchback of Notre Dame*.)

Borgman was first drawn to Rose as a hero, and like many native Cincinnatians remains transfixed by his tragic fall. He takes no pleasure in Pete's current plight, except that it affords him regular opportunities to sketch that singular, spellbinding face.

"Rose was certainly a

> *"For nearly 25 years, I've been trying to arrange 1,000 words worthy of one Borgman cartoon, and there's no surer route to despair."*
>
> Tim Sullivan

MY 25 FAVORITE MOVIES

The Producers
Aguirre, the Wrath of God
Field of Dreams
Manhattan
Cinema Paradiso
Jean de Florette
Manon of the Spring
Raging Bull
Annie Hall
Midnight Cowboy
Pinocchio
Map of the Human Heart
Mad Max
Air Force One
Indiana Jones
and the Temple of Doom
Fargo
Cast Away
Toy Story
The Exorcist
Pulp Fiction
Flirting
Gallipoli
A Thousand Clowns
Taxi Driver
Wag the Dog

disappointment to so many people in this city," Jim says. "That was one big, sad story. I think it's a fallacy to think we in the news love it when things go wrong. I don't like to see the world go wrong. I grew up loving and admiring Pete Rose."

Borgman's attachment to pro football is more tenuous. Though his office window overlooks Paul Brown Stadium, he remembers attending only two Cincinnati Bengals games — one of them on assignment at the Super Bowl.

Distance has its advantages. An artist would call it perspective. From his 19th floor aerie, Borgman almost cannot fail to capture the big picture. His challenge has been to find fresh ways to say futility.

The Bengals have been so lousy for so long that the committee charged with choosing the contents for this book was ultimately compelled to limit the number of variations on the same theme.

Happily, the editors kept Jim's 1979 inspiration: "Little Sisters Of The Poor 77, Bengals 3," as well as its spirited spiritual descendant, the 1994 classic celebrating the furious pass rush of Thelma Spiegelmeier of the St. Barnabas Auxiliary.

Study the detail of the drawing. Thelma has cast away her cane (and lost her glasses) to record her fourth sack of then-Bengals quarterback David Klingler. And if that weren't indignity enough, Borgman shows two of Thelma's elderly teammates closing in unblocked, behind metal walkers.

Studying the cartoon at training camp, almost seven years after it first appeared, Mike Brown begins to giggle.

"I think they're really pretty good," he said, leafing through Borgman's Bengals portfolio. "They make me laugh. But I probably wasn't happy when I saw them for the first time in the paper."

That the old cartoons still seem fresh, so far from the context of current events, is a tribute to Borgman's sense of the absurd and his feel for what's really true and what's merely funny. Much of his best work is high concept — consider the papal procession for Johnny Bench Day — and nearly none of it consists of low comedy. Borgman generally favors the flight of fancy to the pie in the face, eschewing the easy one-liner for more layered laughs or pure poignancy.

"I always compare it to pitching," he said. "If you try to throw fastballs every day, readers will start lining them up the middle at you. You've got to know how to change speeds."

At the top of his game, Jim Borgman is as masterful as Greg Maddux. He makes most of us feel as if we were swinging bats made of balsa.

A SALUTE FROM A COLLEAGUE

Several of Jim's professional colleagues were asked to commemorate his silver anniversary at The Enquirer. *This drawing was created by Jeff Stahler, cartoonist of* The Cincinnati Post.

"... AND WOULD YOU LOOK AT THIS, NUX! HERE COMES THE POPE, ALONG WITH THE ENTIRE COLLEGE OF CARDINALS, FOR THE CANONIZATION CEREMONY AT HOME PLATE!"

September 18, 1983

Johnny Bench has several of my originals, and he gave me an embroidered jacket
when he went into the Hall of Fame. I'll never forget his rifle arm; it just made your jaw drop.

THELMA SPIEGELMEIER OF PRICE HILL RECORDS HER FOURTH SACK in the BIG
St. BARNABAS AUXILIARY UPSET over the BENGALS

September 28, 1994
Listening to my Aunt Jane talk about her card parties at St. Lawrence Church
has paid off with an inexhaustible roster of great Price Hill names.

February 15, 1991
Greed gave baseball fans a sour aftertaste. That feeling peaked after the strike of 1994-95.
For a while, baseball vanished from my cartoons.

August 4, 1978
I loved drawing the young, ruddy Pete Rose. Contrary to myth, we cartoonists
don't enjoy watching heroes crash to earth any more than the average person does.

October 15, 1999
Tall Stacks gives me a chance to draw those big, floating birthday cakes every few years.

"OH, IT LOST A LITTLE MAGIC WHEN RICK PITINO LEFT..."

May 9, 1997
Even if you don't care about basketball, you have to love the passion
with which Kentuckians embrace the Wildcats.

...But there is no joy
in Redsland,
Mighty Tony has
left town.

December 22, 1976
In an era when ballplayers worked their way into a city's heart,
this trade lowered Dick Wagner beyond redemption for most of us.

January 3, 1988
Paul Brown looked like a football coach from central casting.
I liked Forrest Gregg's granite face but Dave Shula, Homer Rice and Sam Wyche were tougher.

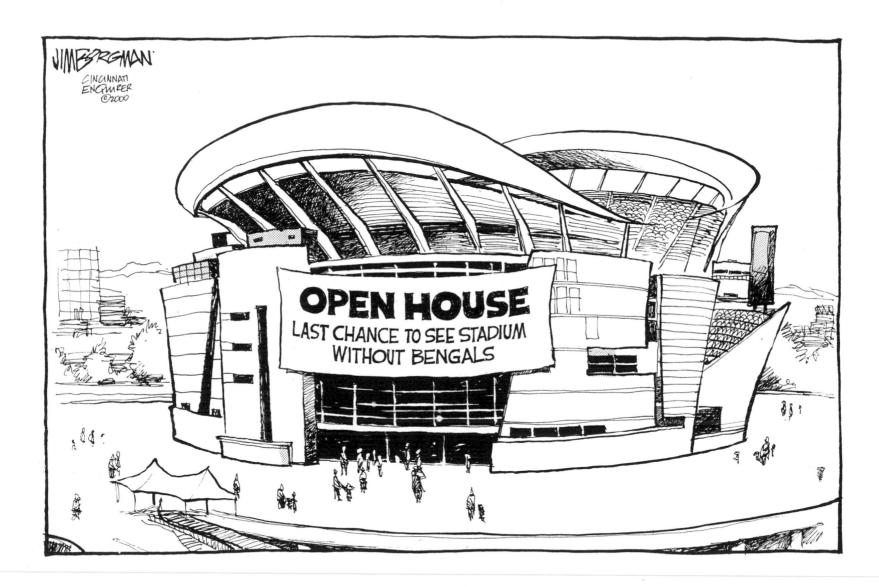

September 1, 2000
Paul Brown Stadium was built right beneath my office window.
I can draw it with my eyes closed, though I've never been inside.

December 18, 1994
I also once drew a goal line around the city of Cincinnati to keep the Bengals from leaving town.

November 25, 1979
One of the first in a long series of Bengals-bashing cartoons. Each year it becomes
more challenging to express the depths of their ineptitude.

NEW MONUMENT UNVEILED ON FOUNTAIN SQUARE

February 14, 2000
After the Reds signed Ken Griffey Jr., Jesus had to settle for the Third Coming.

CARTOON EARNED DISPLAY IN WHITE HOUSE BATHROOM

BY PETER BRONSON

Peter Bronson, associate editor, columnist and editor of **The Enquirer's** *editorial page, joined the newspaper in 1992. A strong conservative, he smilingly describes himself as Jim Borgman's "alleged" boss.*

Ronald Reagan has a face like spoiled fruit rotting under a kiln-hardened, Brylcreamed pompadour. His squinty eyes and toothless bite look just like the old man who terrorized you as a kid when you climbed the neighbor's fence to retrieve your Frisbee. It's that rabid geezer who lunged out of his back door like a moray eel hiding in a coral reef, yelling at the top of his leather lungs, "GET OUTTA MY YARD!"

Americans can identify this guy on sight: It's the scary, mean-spirited, miserly Gipper who made cruel jokes about welfare queens, called those nice Soviets "the evil empire" and proclaimed that henceforth in the Kingdom of Ronald the Terrible, ketchup would be a government-issue vegetable in school lunches, for cryingoutloud.

This is the portrait of Ronald Reagan that greeted the new president just two months after he moved into the White House: A housewarming gift from Jim Borgman.

In the rectangle of newsprint where Jim pulls the wings off politicians, he compared Ronald Reagan to the "before presidency" and "after presidency" caricatures of Lyndon Johnson, Richard Nixon and Jimmy Carter.

The other presidents all aged as gracefully as limburger cheese on the beach in August.

But Mr. Reagan *started out* looking older than dirt under Noah's fingernails. He *started out* more wrinkled than a raisin in a hot tub.

In this March 1980 cartoon, Jim left the "end of term" space for President Reagan blank, leaving it to the reader's horrified imagination to conjure an unspeakable image of decay and dissipation. Maybe just a pile of dust would be all that would remain of Ronald Reagan after a week in office.

Now let's take a look at virile, vital, dynamic, charismatic President Bill Clinton.

The Borgman version is a cross between rib-tickling, rosy-nosed W.C. Fields and the cute Pillsbury Doughboy, a lovable, huggable, big lug of a rogue. Even with his

To Jim Borgman — now America's premier bathroom decorator! Thanks Bill Clinton

President Bill Clinton insisted on showing Jim the place of honor for one of his original cartoons of the president.
It hung in the bathroom just outside the White House Oval Office.

pants down in a police station lineup, he has that endearingly innocent "Who, me?" look of a class clown.

The Jim Borgman Designer Clinton is sometimes sloppy, but he's never mean. He might leer, but he never squints. He howls at the moon, but he doesn't snarl or bite. He's just a scruffy, tail-wagging, clumsy mutt of a president, who chews your best pair of shoes, digs holes in the yard and stains the carpet, then slobbers all over your slacks and gives you those big wet eyes when you roll up the paper to give him a whack.

How could anyone think of taking him to the impeachment pound?

Now, the record shows that Mr. Clinton had a few fleas: Travelgate, Filegate, Whitewater, Chinagate, the Lincoln Bedroom for rent, Waco, the Starr Report, perjury, obstruction of justice, cattle futures, Pardongate, Gennifer, Paula, Monica, Kathleen, Juanita and the majorettes section of the University of Arkansas Marching Band (this is a partial list).

Mr. Reagan had occasional brushes with narcolepsy and something called Iran-Contra, although he claimed he was napping at the time when they woke him up to tell him about it.

So why such extravagantly disparate treatment in

MY 25 FAVORITE NON-CARTOON ARTISTS

Bernini
Kathe Kollwitz
Fritz Scholder
Rembrandt
Gustav Klimt
Michelangelo
Caravaggio
Georges Rouault
Claude Monet
Andrew Wyeth
N.C. Wyeth
John Singer Sargent
Ansel Adams
Robert A. Nelson
Martin Garhart
Pablo Picasso
Wayne Thiebauld
Ben Shahn
Emily Richardson
Annie Leibovitz
Heinrich Kley
Friedensreich Hundertwasser
Claes Oldenburg
Roy Lichtenstein
Jasper Johns

Borgmanland? How did Jim go from President Prune to President Swoon?

To understand the Borgman approach to political cartoons, every unserious nonacademic study like this one should start with these two towering presidents whose ability to

inspire love and loathing dwarfs tedious Carter and beige Bushes.

Examine the artwork. Where Mr. Reagan is all sharp edges and pointy angles, Mr. Clinton is round and circular, like his definition of "is."

Many think it's because Jim is a recidivist liberal. That's true. Jim is so liberal he thinks Al Gore was robbed of the presidency by the Supreme Court, when everyone knows Al Gore was robbed of the presidency by Al Gore. Jim is so liberal he spent his entire Bush tax rebate on Barbra Streisand CDs and a set of *Doonesbury* glassware. He's so liberal he thinks taxes are too low and wants to pay more for foolishly wasteful government programs such as adequate education for children, aid to starving Third World countries and protecting the environment from oil slicks and toxic waste. He's so liberal he thinks artists, including cartoonists, ought to be able to write cuss words and display pictures of naked people, no matter what the local sheriff says. He's so liberal — well, maybe he just looks so liberal because his office is next to mine.

Any guy who draws Saddam Hussein scorched like Elmer Fudd smoking a TNT cigar can't be all bad.

But being a Kennedy/Hillary/McGovern liberal, as sad as it is, is only a tiny corner of the Borgman cartoon picture.

Jim is an incredibly well-informed student of current events. He goes beyond the surface, plunging deep into the details of policy and politics to offer readers sophisticated, thoughtfully nuanced cartoons on very complicated topics that nobody cares about and only a few of us who need to get a life even understand.

If a matchstick floating on a pond represents how deep most of us go into complicated public issues, Jim is at the bottom of the deepest trench in the Pacific, and he needs to come up for air before his hull implodes.

He knows the difference between NAFTA and GATT. He knows how a bill becomes a law. He knows what it is like to be a lifeless policy wonk tangled in the snarled yarn of government bureaucracy. He even knows what "wonk" means, I think, because he created a short-lived cartoon called *Wonk City,* which was beloved by editorial writers and nobody else.

In other words, Jim is not the two-dimensional man you see when he draws himself in a cartoon. He's three-dimensional, just like the rest of us. And he spends an enormous amount of time researching issues, reading scholarly opinions and carefully weighing complex issues before he

takes a position on the wrong side.

And then there's this:

By Jim's admission and as previously related, the truth can be told about Jim's private personal relationship with the president behind closed doors.

In the early days of the Clinton presidency, when pizza boxes were still the only mess the president was getting into and interns wandered the White House unmolested, Mr. Clinton made the most brilliant strategic move of his long and colorful political career. He invited Jim Borgman, the world's most hazardous political cartoonist, to visit the White House.

And there, after a flattering lunch with the president, Mr. Clinton invited Jim to take a private tour of the Oval Office, just the two of them: the Sword and the Pen.

The president turned on the 500-watt Clinton charm, murmured sweet talk and compliments, draped a big paw over Jim's shoulder and steered him into a windowless little hall directly off the Oval Office, a special presidential inner sanctum where, as we learned later, only the most privileged of the president's friends named Monica were invited to join him.

And that's where it happened.

Off the hallway, behind a door, President Clinton directed Jim's eyes to a place on the wall,

directly over the commander in chief's official United States of America presidential commode. Hanging there was a Jim Borgman cartoon of Mr. Clinton — enshrined in a place of unprecedented presidential honor.

One can only speculate what all this might have triggered in the dizzied mind of a political cartoonist. It's a profession not known for a lot of subtlety.

George Bush 43 might say, "The subliminable message was flashing like a neutron billboard."

And his father would say, "Suck-up city."

From that point forward, Bill Clinton became one of Jim's most beloved cartoon subjects. Which is not entirely a positive thing.

President Ronald Reagan celebrated his 76th birthday with the national press by displaying a birthday drawing by Jim. Mrs. Reagan, partially shown, helps hold the drawing.

So what about the scary, shriveled husk that was Borgman's daffy President Reagan? What happened here?

Only Jim's friends know the truth, and none of them told me. But I heard that when Jim was 6, he was badly frightened by a movie starring Ronald Reagan as a man who loses both legs, and wakes up in bed screaming, "Where is the rest of me!?"

Jim was traumatized, and to this day he has had an unreasoning fear that Republicans will amputate spending while America sleeps.

I know all of this for a fact because I just made it up.

Here's another true fact: Out of a dozen cartoons on politics chosen for this book, half are about Bill Clinton, which is 50 percent less than Bill Clinton wanted and 50 percent more than Ken Starr wanted.

There are few about George Bush Sr. His presidency did not register on Borgman radar except for a stick-figure vice president who could not spell potatoe.

George Bush II makes an appearance, looking too small for the presidential desk and chair, like a kid visiting daddy's office.

Some readers resent this. They complain that Mr. Bush is not getting equal attention in Borgman cartoons.

They are misguided. Getting attention in a Borgman cartoon is like asking to spend more "quality time" with your dentist or demanding equal opportunity to participate in an IRS audit.

What many readers fail to realize is that politicians want attention from political cartoonists the way wagon trains wanted attention from the Apaches. The more "fun" cartoonists are having with President Luke Warm, the more likely President Luke Warm is in a miserable mess that is making national headlines that include lots of words that end in "gate."

I know all this because I pretend to be Jim's boss and he pretends he has one.

I also pretend people read the editorials we write, when I know they only turn to our section to see what Borgman is doing.

Jim pretends to take our endorsements seriously when he knows that he can make a complete mockery of our candidate by drawing him with food stuck in his teeth.

All this is nearly as annoying as trying to disagree with someone who is one of the nicest, most likable and funniest people I have ever had the pleasure to work with.

I asked Jim to share his opinions about drawing presidents, because I thought this

section should include something that is not made up.

"Reagan and Clinton are my favorite presidents to draw — I missed Nixon's heyday by a hair — because they both had larger-than-life presidencies," he replied.

"When you're cartooning, it helps to have a president with a strong stance to react to, push off of. Reagan was best that way: He took strong, clear positions and usually expressed them colorfully, so he was easy to respond to. Too, he had an expressive face — that jaw that jutted out when he was angry, the eyes that crinkled when he was amused, or confused. His handlers set him in colorful locations — flag factories, national parks — to deliver policy statements, so there was always something visual to take off from. His administration laid out the buffet, and all you had to do was come fill your plate. That's as good as it gets.

"Clinton was good for different reasons. Like Nixon, the complexity of his personality, needs, grand visions and base desires made him a national character study, and there always seemed to be new layers to mine. His ideological squishiness would have made him tough to draw about — a constantly moving target — had he not handed us such gaudy material

> *"In other words, Jim is not the two-dimensional man you see when he draws himself in a cartoon. He's three-dimensional, just like the rest of us."*
> Peter Bronson

WHERE IDEAS COME FROM...

WHERE JIM'S IDEAS COME FROM.

to work with in his second term.

"At the end of the day, sometimes despite logic, I liked Clinton because I felt he understood and sympathized with the little guys. I distrusted Reagan because I never felt he did. So sue me.

"For the same reason, Bush 41 was hard work. He told us he hated broccoli, and we had the dual citizenship thing — Kennebunkport and Texas — but that's thin pickings. His stock is going up retroactively for raising a walking, talking malaprop who may turn into a good president yet. For us cartoonists, that is.

"If any of this helps, use it."

Yes, it helps, but actually I was hoping for a little more, so my part would be to write, "Jim Borgman says," and go home early.

But this way, Jim gets the last laugh. Cartoonists always do, because the pen is mightier than the word.

A SALUTE FROM A COLLEAGUE

Several of Jim's professional colleagues were asked to commemorate his silver anniversary at The Enquirer. *This drawing was created by Dave Coverly, creator of the comic strip* Speed Bump.

March 27, 1980
When Ronald Reagan became the oldest candidate to seek the presidency, it seemed reasonable
to consider the toll it might take on him. Ironically, he weathered the eight years, looking even younger than when he began.

April 12, 1992
Newly elected President Clinton invited some editorial cartoonists to the Oval Office, and
when I introduced myself, he said, "I know you. I have one of your cartoons hanging in the bathroom." This is it.

August 22, 1999
Presidential campaigns can be a field day as cartoonists get to know the new players.

December 10, 2000
During the contested election of 2000, I drew separate cartoons for each candidate as a winner.
They collected dust until I finally tipped my hand and showed each to our readers.

February 26, 2001
A big figure like Bill Clinton is hard to get off the stage.
He's one of those complex characters Americans can't stop watching.

November 6, 1996
Watching the Clinton presidency was like watching the Indy 500, hoping/not hoping for a crash.

February 21, 2001
George W. barely disguised the fact that he has a score to settle for Pop.

December 15, 2000
Antonin Scalia tipped the election to George W. Bush and all illusions of a non-partisan Supreme Court collapsed.

January 16, 1995
For two years I did a weekly comic strip about Beltway politics called *Wonk City*
at the request of Meg Greenfield for the *Washington Post*.

November 2, 1983
I confess I'd vote for a Colin Powell, Joe Lieberman or Elizabeth Dole
despite political differences just to break the race/religion/sex barriers.

February 11, 2001
When I saw Hannibal Lecter in his mask in movie previews, I knew I'd have to find
an excuse to draw him. President Clinton was generous in providing such opportunities.

June 1, 1997
Paula Jones gave comedians a chance to air their white-trash jokes. The rawdriness of it all was overwhelming. A reader gave me an idea I
loved (and used). It showed the White House limo bearing the bumper sticker, "If this limo's rockin', don't come a-knockin'."

My Dad Headed To Alaska Yelling 'Mush, You Huskies!'

By Dylan Borgman

Dylan Borgman, 18, spent a week in August 2001 with his dad, driving a VW Beetle to Pomona College in California where he is a freshman. He was graduated from Walnut Hills High School.

Dad's sabbatical was a promise to himself. When he first started at the *Enquirer,* he vowed that midway through his career, he would take a break. It took him several years to plan and save for the event. It began on March 1, 1993 and ended on Dec 1.

But when the final decision was made, everything took on an eerie silence. One day, my dad left his office and didn't return for nine months. Many people were shocked and surprised. Not me. Even at my young age, I knew what a sabbatical meant — a summer vacation. My dad was going on a summer vacation. I merely thought of it as his chance to go to exotic places

and to sit at home and watch soap operas.

Most of his vacation was spent doing things at the house. It wasn't much of a change in my life. He would be there when I left for school, and there when I came back. I assume he didn't spend the time in between watching soap operas. Most of the time was spent working on household projects, thinking, doodling and reading.

He cut himself off from the news. In our house, there were no 6 o'clock news programs, no newspapers, nor any conversations about world events. People would ask him about what he thought about the current crisis in Washington and he would just shrug. It wasn't a

major effort to isolate himself from newsmakers for a while.

Indeed, when he did return, that generated one of the biggest differences in his work. Being given a chance to separate himself from his work allowed him to gain perspective. Most people, he learned, don't care about Zoning Bill 3292 or whatever the daily news item is. Most people are concerned with things that affect their lives. That's when he began doing more and more "domestic" cartoons, that is, cartoons that depict normal people in their everyday lives.

I suppose he began to see the news from a guy-on-the-street perspective. But don't think for a minute that Dad receded into a

Susan Butcher, Iditarod race champion, made this photo of Jim on his journey across northern Alaska.

corner of his house for his sabbatical.

In a brash and unexpected display of courage, Dad hopped on a plane for Alaska to go dogsledding. The whole trip was conceived when he met Susan Butcher — perhaps the world's greatest dogsledding champion — at an awards banquet several months earlier. They seemed to click and, soon enough, she was inviting him to come mushing in Alaska. I'm sure that, at the time, he had no idea that this was actually going to happen. It was just conversation.

The following May, he was in Barrow, Alaska, being dragged across icy tundra.

After a couple of hours of "training" in which he was told to hang on to the sled as Susan and her aides tipped and rocked it, they deemed him ready for the long trip to Prudhoe Bay. My dad has all sorts of inspirational stories to tell about those days on the sled. Before his departure, they gave him a rifle in case he encountered polar bears. Perhaps the bear would use the gun's barrel to pick its teeth after it ate him. Dad believed the dogsled party was going to travel in a tight pack, one sled right in front of

> *"Before his departure, they gave him a rifle in case he encountered polar bears. Perhaps the bear would use the gun's barrel to pick its teeth after it ate him."*
>
> Dylan Borgman

25 Things I Like About My Dad

By Chelsea Borgman

He is always there for me
He never misses a chance to sleep
in front of the TV
He deals with our three dogs
He'll always watch the *Rugrats* with me
He is willing to redo my bathroom for me
He will order pizza at 11 PM
He will offer to go for ice cream
without my asking
He is always watching out for me
He is either early or late, not on time
He buys me exactly what I wanted
He always wants to go for a bike ride
He tries not to embarrass me, I think
He is nice to my friends
He lets me have sleepovers at the
spur of the moment
He will always read with me
He does not pretend to like doing the bills
He always finds time for me
He listens to me
He is not a workaholic
He is willing to buy 'N Sync everything
He cries along with my friends
during *My Dog Skip*
He helps my friends and me
build the best fort ever!
He helps me with my homework
He lets me color some of his comic strips
He believes in me

the other. Actually, the sleds spread themselves over hundreds of feet. Most of the time, he didn't see them at all. During whiteouts, he couldn't tell the sky from the ground and he found himself in an existential void of nothingness.

Fortunately, he had a song stuck in his memory for moments like this. For the entire trip from Barrow, Alaska, to Prudhoe Bay, the Mr. Rogers song "You Can Never Go Down The Drain" repeated over and over in his mind.

This is what he said he learned from his trip:

First of all, trust your dogs because they're loyal to Susan and will keep pulling you through no matter how far you are into the white wilderness. In other words, you can never go down the drain.

And second, never let go of your sled. If you do, the dogs will think it's their lucky day and keep running. There you'll be, in a world where the sun shines 24 hours a day and you can't tell the sky from the ground.

My dad took a mental picture of himself out there. When he's at home, sitting in front of that drawing table in his office, that picture will remind him of the farthest he has ever gotten to the edge of the void.

To be fair, most of his life isn't

Syndicated cartoonist Jeff MacNelly, creator of the comic strip *Shoe*, hailed
Jim's return from his sabbatical with this special drawing.

Jim prepared this drawing for King Features, which syndicates his work,
and the syndicate used it in a promotion welcoming him back to work.

spent searching out adventure in the wild unknown. The person I know is the one who sits in our living room, reading *Harry Potter* to my sister. He loved doing things like that for me when I was her age as well. We read the entire series of the Doctor Dolittle books when I was between the ages of 6 and 9.

Cartoonists are notoriously informal. Dad used to go to the *Enquirer* wearing a leather vest and a clean white dress shirt and a tie, but a couple of dozen awards later, the cartoonist I know switched to less formal attire. He wears a paper-thin, long-sleeved shirt that might not come off for 19-hour increments. I haven't ever touched that shirt.

Our house feels big and empty these days without my mother, Lynn, but we are always busy with something or other. My dad spends late nights up in his office working on strips. I'll often poke my head in the door and talk to him about whatever's on my mind. Sometimes he'll call upon me to help him with his 7-year-old computer which, I believe, was made when they were still using punch cards to program them. My job in the family is to be the tech guy. Some of that comes out in the comic strip *Zits*. We have three computers and my job is to go around and perform voodoo on them so that my dad can send his comic strips to the

right people on time and for my sister to be able to play her video game, The Sims, all day long.

We have three dogs in our household. My dad loves each one dearly. This summer as I prepared to go to college, he leaned over to me at the dinner table and said in a very serious voice: "A few days after you arrive in Pomona College, you're going to receive a very large box with holes in it. It will contain two, possibly three, animals which are now yours."

OK, he doesn't love them *dearly*. It is my sister who keeps him from putting the dogs in the woods to go live like the wild animals they are. The first two dogs were my mother's idea so she could have companionship around our house. When the first dog, Mulder, didn't live up to her hopes, she then talked Dad into a second dog. After Mom died, my sister somehow managed to get a third dog into our house. I love watching Dad and the dogs interact because he tries to reason with them, as if they understand what he is saying. I think they bring our family closer together in an unspoken way.

Of course, the death of my mother also aided in knitting us closer together. Mom died suddenly from complications in surgery around two years ago. After that, it became important

to prove that we could still live normal lives as a family. We began going on family trips together. We started out small with a trip to Red River Gorge. Since then, we have visited California, Sweden, Finland, Florida and Italy. I think it keeps us in good spirits about our functionality as a family.

One of my favorite memories of that sabbatical year was our trip to Santa Fe. My mother has always been in love with New Mexico; so when Dad went on his break, we planned a long road trip to Santa Fe with stop-offs all over the country. I spent most of the trip in the back of our van, lying on the floor, trying to avoid the heat; but I do remember going to Arches National Park in Utah. Arches is an expansive park with nothing but red sand and monumental rock formations. Dad put my sister, who was very young at the time, in a little backpack and we went hiking all over the landscape. I remember those times because it's when I can remember my dad being the most happy in his life. He seemed adventuresome and liberated.

You could tell he was taking everything in. I think that's what his sabbatical was really about: It was a chance to escape the office and go play in the great unknown with his loved ones.

"A few days after you arrive in Pomona College, you're going to receive a very large box with holes in it. It will contain two, possibly three, animals which are now yours."

Jim to
Dylan Borgman

BETTER TO BE A BARKING DOG THAN JUST A 'NICE' MAN

BY LEE ANN HAMILTON

Cincinnati native Lee Ann Hamilton remained a Jim Borgman fan while working at USA Today and the Jackson (MS) Clarion-Ledger. She is The Enquirer's assistant managing editor for enterprise.

In Jim Borgman's world, assisted-suicide doc Jack Kevorkian is so scary he gives the Grim Reaper the creeps. Americans are so bamboozled by modern medical miracles that Gulliblexx is the newest wonder drug. So many people have left Cincinnati for the suburbs that they're hauling downtown's Tyler-Davidson Fountain out there with them.

There's nothing really deep about commenting on social issues of the day, Jim says.

"The editorial cartoonist's job is to be a dog barking in the night," he says. "You bark at intruders and squirrels that pass by. It's your job to alert others to movement in the yard."

He doesn't have to nail all the bad guys or solve all the world's problems. "You're not always going to identify the intruders," he says, "but you serve a useful role by alerting people they're there."

More than 7,500 cartoons since he began, Jim barks at the absurdities of doctors, lawyers, judges, journalists and the goofy people next door. He yaps at trash TV and Internet porn. He whimpers about e-mail, e-commerce, e-shopping, e-novels, e-parking, e-addictions and even e-Santa. He howls loudest at gun laws that fail to protect kids from the bad judgment of adults.

"Jim lives with America. And I'm jealous of that," says partner and colleague Jerry Scott, co-creater with Jim of the *Zits* cartoon strip. The characters in Jim's editorial cartoons are big, doughy Midwesterners just like him — not the self-absorbed, whacked-out birds from California, where Scott works and lives.

"He's got a liberal bent, but he's more than a political cartoonist," Scott says. "I would describe him as a moral cartoonist. He cares about families and kids, and he does not like guns."

Social commentary, Jim says, is a running conversation with readers, an attempt to connect with the "basic, universal human reaction to what's going on in the world."

"Daily cartooning is like a daily dialogue, a new little thought to throw into the stew that you're boiling," he says. "You ride the debate along. You can't have a definitive answer. And that's very much the spirit I bring to it."

Along the way, Jim ridicules the inane in us all: "It's simple," a dim-witted woman explains to her friend. "I just dial 10-10-967883324589000 and save 10 cents a minute by completely forgetting who I was going to call."

He champions the little guy: "Eldon Flagler was awarded the Nobel Prize for medicine today for discovering how to get his HMO to pay for an overnight hospital stay following quadruple bypass surgery."

And in a world that questions where and when life even begins, he cuts through the imponderable: "My oldest was an all-natural delivery," says the proud mom pushing a baby buggy. "Then Freddy was Caesarean, Jenny was in-vitro, and the twins came freeze-dried in their own resealable, zip-lock storage bags."

Jim routinely jabs at the nation's courts for the lengths to which they will go. "Here's an interesting case," a man reading the newspaper tells his bewildered wife. "Do grandparents have the right to see their grandchildren other than when they're selling raffle tickets, magazines or Girl Scout cookies?"

Perhaps no subject is as clear-cut as gun control. Jim is a fervent advocate, a conclusion based not on any one event in his life, but on years of mounting evidence that guns kill.

"I'll give up my gun when they pry it from my kid's cold, dead fingers," he says in a cartoon that starkly depicts a child's lifeless hand next to a smoking gun. In another, the little boy tells the little girl by the open drawer in his parents' bedroom, "And this is where my dad keeps the gun that we don't know about."

"It's rare to find an issue that you feel so clear about that you can just hammer away," Jim says. The downside is knowing that every cartoon frame will be scrutinized and criticized by millions.

"That's where the argument goes nowhere," he says. "There is a feeling of spitting in the wind. People know whether they are for or against it. There are people who agree, but there are people who came up with a different attitude, like hunters, who have just as strong a visceral reaction as I have."

No subject is taboo, although many are murky, Jim says. Take the world's fascination with human genetic engineering and cloning.

"I don't know what I think about all that," Jim says. "It really does come down to: Do we trust ourselves to be tinkering in this area?"

Don't try pinning Jim down to any neat and tidy editorial philosophy, either. If he seems liberal and anti-establishment one day, he is. The next he may be pro-police and law-and-order and equally as loud.

"I'm not a knee-jerk liberal, although readers in this town tend to see me this way," he says. "I do have a conservative streak — call it cautious level-headedness."

He's also been known to change his mind about things. Welfare reform that shook millions of Americans from the rolls didn't turn out so bad after all, he says. "I thought we were going to find the streets littered with people living in boxes, but to a great extent, that didn't materialize.

"I don't find particular embarrassment around calling a shot wrong," he says. "It's just a good thing I don't run the world."

If anything, Jim has a sweet spot for kids and people who have to fight for things in life. "I just have a lot of sympathy and empathy for people who weren't born six feet tall and who have some strike against them going out in the world."

He's also sweet on Cincinnati, which makes the lampoons of his hometown all the more real. And local issues are just more fun, he

"He's got a liberal bent, but he's more than a political cartoonist. I would describe him as a moral cartoonist. He cares about families and kids, and he does not like guns."
Jerry Scott

says, because readers have more reaction to them.

Cartoons on the Bengals are always crowd-pleasers, especially when they're losing football games to the Little Sisters of the Poor. More controversial cartoons depict the poor-performing Cincinnati Public Schools as a skeleton covered in Band-aids. Four months after the April 2001 race riots, Jim exposed the folly of a city still in denial of racial problems. He drew ostriches, their heads in the sand, as a fitting sequel to the Summer of 2000's Big Pig Gig, in which 425 ceramic painted pigs lolled about town.

"I don't know what to do about AIDS in Africa, but I can try to help the folks in our city get along from one day to the next," Jim says.

He's not apt to draw a cartoon simply to provoke a reaction, though. "My opinions are all pretty genuine. I don't intend to outrage just to outrage," he says. "You really do have to be able to say what's on your mind if you want it to have any kind of power."

MY 25 FAVORITE BOOKS

Catcher in the Rye / J.D. Salinger
Kolymsky Heights / Lionel Davidson
Angela's Ashes / Frank McCourt
The Gift / Lewis Hyde
A Grief Observed / C.S. Lewis
The Hobbit / J.R.R. Tolkien
The Boys of Summer / Roger Kahn
Watership Down / Richard Adams
The Sound and The Fury / William Faulkner
Smilla's Sense of Snow / Peter Hoeg
Huckleberry Finn / Mark Twain
A Soldier of the Great War / Mark Helprin
*In the Heart of the Heart
of the Country* / William Gass
Care of the Soul / Thomas Moore
The Road Less Traveled / M. Scott Peck
Lord of the Flies / William Golding
The Big Sky / A.B. Guthrie
The Greatest of Marlys / Lynda Barry
Winnie the Pooh / A. A. Milne
Grapes of Wrath / John Steinbeck
In Cold Blood / Truman Capote
The Father / Sharon Olds
To Kill a Mockingbird / Harper Lee
Harry Potter and the Sorcerer's Stone / J.K. Rowling
Winterdance / Gary Paulsen

A 1995 cartoon may be the most personal Jim ever created. To this day, he rarely draws himself in his work. Yet in six frames titled "One Story About Being White in Cincinnati," he caricatured himself, first working at his drawing board, then having an interview with a prospective landlady, and finally, walking away from a promising

new home.

"I remember looking for my first apartment when I came back here after college. There was this place down by the river, half of a duplex, that was kind of nice," he says in the first frame.

"When I sat down with the landlady to talk about the details, she said something that made my heart lodge in my throat. 'I'm glad to rent to a nice man like you instead of, you know, one of the coloreds.'

"I remember that I just sat there, didn't say anything, just started looking for the fastest way to get out of there and never come back. I remember being polite and hating myself for it. I think it was because she had just called me a 'nice man.'

"I've always wished I'd told her, 'I won't rent from you, either.' Then stood up and walked out. I've practiced that scene in my mind over and over since then.

"But racism doesn't seem to come at me straight on like that anymore. It's always camouflaged and between the lines. And I'm a block away before I recognize what it was.

*LUXURY — SIMPLE
UNALLOYED LUXURY!*

*I TOLD YA WE SHOULDA
SIGNED-UP WITH BORGMAN YEARS AGO*

Copyright characters Warner Bros.

A SALUTE FROM A COLLEAGUE

Several of Jim's professional colleagues were asked to commemorate his silver anniversary at The Enquirer. *This drawing was created by Chuck Jones, motion-picture animator and creator of the Road Runner.*

"One thing I'm straight about, though, I don't want to be a 'nice man' anymore."

Mostly, Jim wants to be a cartoonist whose work is thoughtful, clear and direct. He tries to treat even the most subtle, nuanced subjects with respect and clarity. He hates it when his message is misunderstood, which is always possible in a medium that daily depends on a one-frame drawing and an average 10 words to express complex thoughts.

"That's why I stare at the paper with blood on my forehead," he says. "I can't stand to oversimplify my thoughts."

Ideas come from hours of reading *The Cincinnati Enquirer* and *New York Times,* skimming through magazines and listening to National Public Radio and the late-night TV talk shows. Readers, too, offer up plenty of suggestions. While Jim listens to them all on voice mail, he probably doesn't use more than one in 20.

"And even then, probably not in the way they intended," he says. "There's something about hearing an idea from somebody else that makes it, well, uninteresting."

On his best days, you can find Jim lost in space, daydreaming as if he hasn't got a clue in the world. But that's exactly the time he's testing ideas and sorting thoughts, the most crucial part of his day. When he's down to his final drawings, and actually looks as if he's working, colleagues could throw the wildest party in his office and it wouldn't distract him a bit.

October 25, 1979
What if schools got all the money they needed and Mike Brown
had to hold a bake sale to sign a linebacker?

April 9, 1989
The idea of a pristine wilderness somewhere on this malled-and-sprawled planet is important to me.
It's painful to think of Prince William Sound (and now the North Slope of Alaska) as just another doormat for polluters.

May 16, 1997
It may be trash, but it's legal. On the other hand, it may be legal, but it's trash.

March 21, 1995
I don't know if a world run by women would be a utopia, but wouldn't it be refreshing to study?

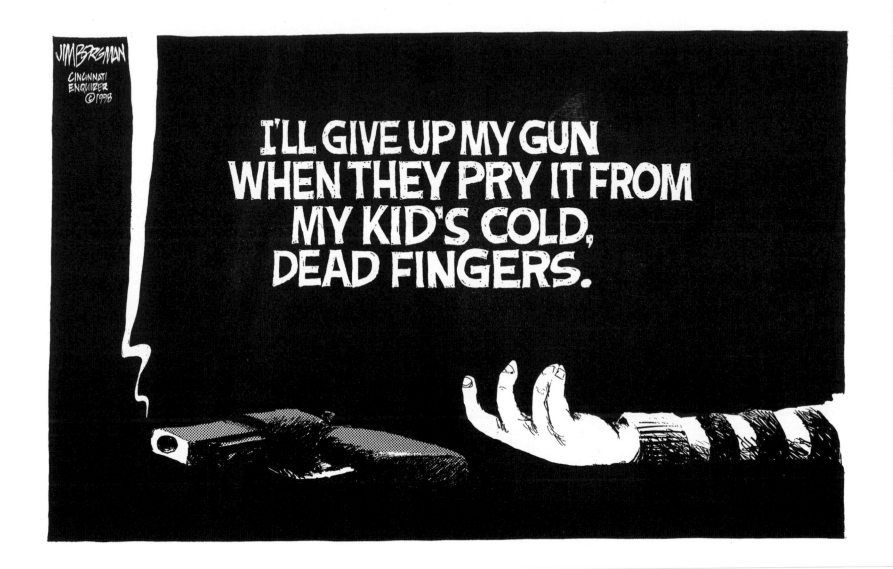

April 21, 1998
Guns don't kill children; parents with unlocked guns kill children.

"...AND THIS IS WHERE MY DAD KEEPS THE GUN THAT WE DON'T KNOW ABOUT."

March 14, 2001
I have little quarrel with the pro-gun individuals who call to argue with me. Most sound
responsible and reasonable. The sheer proliferation of guns, however, leads to so much heartache.

"HONEY, WHY IS IT THAT I FIND YOU IN HERE EVERY NIGHT AFTER YOU WATCH THE NEWS....?"

April 27, 1999
One of the occupational hazards of a life immersed in journalism
is the occasional need to get into bed and pull the covers over your head.

December 29, 1998
Agree or disagree with assisted suicide, Jack Kevorkian was one disturbing champion of the cause.

February 12, 1981
When group homes for the mentally retarded were instituted in Cincinnati, the epicenter of the local debate
was Stettinius Avenue in Hyde Park. People who considered themselves progressive suddenly turned territorial.

"I'M NOT READY FOR THE 'NINETIES! I STILL CAN'T EVEN OPERATE THE VCR!"

December 29, 1989
A decade later, substitute the words "DVD player, instant messenger, Palm Pilot, cell phone ..."

ONE STORY ABOUT BEING WHITE

JIM BORGMAN
CINCINNATI
ENQUIRER
©1995

I REMEMBER LOOKING FOR MY FIRST APARTMENT WHEN I CAME BACK HOME AFTER COLLEGE.

THERE WAS THIS PLACE DOWN BY THE RIVER, HALF OF A DUPLEX, THAT WAS KIND OF NICE.

WHEN I SAT DOWN WITH THE LANDLADY TO TALK ABOUT THE DETAILS, SHE SAID SOMETHING THAT MADE MY HEART LODGE IN MY THROAT

I'M GLAD TO RENT TO A NICE MAN LIKE YOU INSTEAD OF, YOU KNOW, ONE OF THE COLOREDS.

I REMEMBER THAT I JUST SAT THERE, DIDN'T SAY ANYTHING, JUST STARTED LOOKING FOR THE FASTEST WAY TO GET OUT OF THERE AND NEVER COME BACK.

I REMEMBER BEING POLITE AND HATING MYSELF FOR IT.

I THINK IT WAS BECAUSE SHE HAD JUST CALLED ME A 'NICE MAN.'

I'VE ALWAYS WISHED I'D TOLD HER, 'I WON'T RENT FROM YOU EITHER.' THEN STOOD UP AND WALKED OUT.

JUST STAND UP AND WALK OUT, MAN. JUST STAND UP AND WALK OUT.

I'VE PRACTICED THAT SCENE IN MY MIND OVER AND OVER SINCE THEN.

BUT RACISM DOESN'T SEEM TO COME AT ME STRAIGHT ON LIKE THAT ANYMORE. IT'S ALWAYS CAMOUFLAGED AND BETWEEN THE LINES, AND I'M A BLOCK AWAY BEFORE I RECOGNIZE WHAT IT WAS.

ONE THING I AM STRAIGHT ABOUT, THOUGH....

I DON'T WANT TO BE A 'NICE MAN' ANYMORE.

June 4, 1995
When Cincinnati's racial tensions flared, I felt a need to step out from behind my stage curtain and to tell a true story in my own voice. It was my way of looking the reader in the eye, trying to reach a new level of candor.

May 23, 1999
Over the years I've found that my cartoons are more often about the issues closest to home.

TRIBUTES HELP ARTIST SHARE IN COMMUNITY'S GRIEF

BY SARA PEARCE

Sara Pearce is The Enquirer's assistant managing editor for Features and online. She never stops trying to cajole Jim into drawing for the Features sections. She owns a number of original cartoons by Jim — all purchased at pre-Pulitzer prices.

On the morning of September 11, 2001, Jim was glued to the television set in his home studio. It was tuned to CNN.

Like millions of other people around the country, he was staring in disbelief at the devastation unfolding before his eyes. The World Trade Center's twin towers were crashing to the ground in New York City. The Pentagon had been hit in Washington, D.C.

But unlike other people, Jim had to figure out how to express the horror of the moment in a single drawing. How to capture the outrage and shock while memorializing those who had been killed in the terrorist attack.

He was facing an editorial cartoonist's biggest challenge: the obituary cartoon.

That's what cartoonists call these drawings.

No matter how you say it — obituary car*toon*, obitu*ary* cartoon, *obitu*ary cartoon — it's a phrase that doesn't sound right.

But think about it.

How better to broach life's only inescapable action? To express sorrow? To sum up a person in a glance? Especially when drawing cartoons is what you *do*.

The images here are indelible. The Statue of Liberty hunches over amid clouds of dust and debris. Both hands cover her face in grief. Her torch at her feet. Manhattan no longer visible behind her.

Young "John-John" Kennedy crawls into a darkened nook under St. Peter's vast, ornate desk.

A dapper Fred Astaire blithely dances next to a crystal chandelier on the ceiling of heaven's reception office.

The great humanitarian nun Mother Teresa is hugged and, in turn, enfolds an emaciated God in her expansive arms.

Death provides an editorial cartoonist's most unique effort — and only the best cartoonists create instantly recognizable, universally understood images that not only withstand time but grow more meaningful with it. A drawing of Dr. Martin Luther King extinguishing the flames of racism is powerful even though it was drawn years after his death.

During periods of mourning, these knowing images pull people together. They comfort, console and, sometimes, even make us laugh.

Laugh? Sure.

"Humor is a basic drive and far more serious than it is humorous," says Ray Brown, professor of pop culture emeritus at Bowling Green State University. "And what could be more serious than death? To be treated with whimsy is to make it more bearable, to touch upon the depths and lessen the horror."

Death "makes me fully aware of the power of cartooning," Jim says as he sits at his drawing table rifling through the obituary cartoons stacked in front of him. "Not to be morbid, but so often my job calls for inflammatory comments, and these give me a chance to think about someone's life story, to step back a little ... and I enjoy that."

That's only natural, says Lucy Shelton Caswell, curator of The Ohio State University Cartoon Research Library. "When a community — defined however you want to, as the city of Cincinnati, as the U.S.A., as the world community — mourns the loss of someone, it isn't surprising that the editorial cartoonist sees this as an appropriate arena for commentary."

She views it as the cartoonist's way of sharing in the community's grief and of "personally" marking the loss.

Look through these cartoons and there is no mistaking how personal they are. Jim pours his own emotions and, yes, opinions, into them.

So, St. Peter relays a question from God to the liberal Supreme Court Justice Thurgood Marshall: "He wants to know, 'Can you get used to writing the majority opinion?'..." Jim laughs and says "I enjoyed implying that heaven is ruled by liberals."

Ted Berry, Cincinnati's first African-American mayor, is memorialized in a stark, heroic portrait and the words: "In those days there were giants ..."

Jim's closeness to the subjects makes it simple for him to recall exactly how he went about creating each cartoon. Some came easier than others.

"The best is when you visually remember a great moment in someone's life, like Fred Astaire dancing on the ceiling (as he did in the 1951 movie *Royal Wedding*), a visual that everyone associates with that person that you can tweak a little bit."

So Jim "Peanut Jim" Shelton sits in a wheelchair next to his peanut cart outside the gates of heaven — just as he sat in a wheelchair next to his cart outside the gates of Crosley Field and near Riverfront Stadium for half a century.

Lucy, Charles Schulz's grumpy "Peanuts" character, kneels on an empty field, holding a football and waiting to yank it out from under Charlie Brown's foot one more time. She lets out a single sigh — an indication that she knows what the reader knows: that Charlie will never show. (Not because, at the time, Mr. Schulz was dead, but because he had announced his retirement and the end — in effect, the death — of the comic strip).

A girl sleeps beneath a plump quilt in a distinctly Seussian setting. The bed's headboard is a maze of curlicues. The landscape outside the window is filled with soft, rolling hills, gangly trees and misshapen bushes. At the foot of her bed, the Cat in the Hat's signature hat is perched atop an open book by Dr. Seuss.

Another child offers an apple up to a black, star- and planet-studded sky in a poignant homage to Christa McAuliffe, the New Hampshire high school teacher who died aboard the space shuttle Challenger when it exploded shortly after liftoff on Jan. 28, 1986. Jim remembers the moment well. "We were not expecting to be drawing a cartoon about a tragedy," he says while looking at the simple, yet

"The best is when you visually remember a great moment in someone's life, like Fred Astaire dancing on the ceiling (as he did in the 1951 movie Royal Wedding, a visual that everyone associates with that person that you can tweak a little bit."

Jim Borgman

haunting, cartoon.

"I drew it and redrew it and redrew it," he says. In his head, he had the familiar image of a child's hand offering an apple to a teacher. But he couldn't get the hand right.

"I looked at reference books like *100 Hands*. I looked in the mirror trying to draw my own hand. Finally, almost in desperation, I decided to draw it as a child would draw a hand." It clicked. "And that allowed me to make outer space more loose, more childlike.

"I had four versions before this and they all missed."

The cartoon that finally felt right transformed an everyday image into an image that is achingly compelling and into a cartoon that was cathartic for both artist and reader.

But Jim is the first person to acknowledge that he doesn't always get it right. Just ask him about popcorn pitchman Orville Redenbacher. "That was in truly bad taste," he says, then winces at the thought of it. "I had him being cremated ... with popcorn coming out ... I don't know what I was thinking!"

Sometimes, more than a single cartoon is called for, says Jim. When Cincinnati police officers Daniel Pope and Ronald Jeter were shot to death in December 1997, Jim drew two cartoons. The first depicted the city as a

> *"If it is something that occupies the city for a while, as these shootings did, I feel that there needs to be more than one cartoon. After all, the mission of these is communal, to provide a bonding moment."*
>
> Jim Borgman

MY 25 FAVORITE CARTOONISTS

Mort Drucker
Chuck Jones
Walt Kelly
Bill Watterson
Jerry Scott
Lynda Barry
Mike Peters
Jeff MacNelly
Pat Oliphant
Patrick McDonnell
Charles Schulz
Ben Katchor
George Herrimann
Mike Luckovich
Lynn Johnston
Jeff Stahler
Rube Goldberg
Robert Crumb
Phil Frank
James Stevenson
George Booth
Dave Coverly
Gary Larson
Ronald Searle
Ralph Steadman

man (Cincin) and a woman (nati), heads bowed, at the feet of the police memorial statue with the words "Death in the family" below a bouquet of flowers.

The second, published here, has a policeman standing in front of a flag-draped casket. Underneath are the words: " ... but deliver us from evil. Amen."

"If it is something that occupies the city for a while, as these shootings did, I feel that there needs to be more than one cartoon," Jim says. "After all, the mission of these is communal, to provide a bonding moment."

Lucy Caswell agrees. Obituary cartoons, she says, "succinctly express a community's grief."

He also drew cartoon after cartoon to play out the stages of the nation's grief after the New York and Washington, D.C., attacks. The first day's disquieting Statue of Liberty was followed the next day by a defiant image of the tattered American flag with a snippet from the "Star-Spangled Banner" above it: "... and the flag was still there." The third cartoon was one of anger, showing a clenched fist with the words "... and deliver evil from us."

Each cartoon captured a different moment and reflected Jim's sense of the changing reactions — the leap from shock to sadness to anger — as the story unfolded. As he drew the Statue of Liberty, he knew that he would not show her — as other cartoonists did — on her knees, sitting down or collapsed. "I wanted to show her standing, body language is important ... I wanted to show that we are not on our knees."

Although he had not yet drawn the fourth cartoon when

A SALUTE FROM A COLLEAGUE

Several of Jim's professional colleagues were asked to commemorate his silver anniversary at The Enquirer. *This drawing was created by Patrick McDonnell, creator of the comic strip* Mutts.

A GENIE IN THE BOTTLE!

JEANNIE!!?! IT LOOKS LIKE JIM.

HAPPY 25th ANNIVERSARY!!

MANY MORE ——.
PATRICK McDONNELL
©2001

we talked, he already knew it would be about "funerals and memorials and prayers — and I will try to hit a tone that is right for that. I am going through this as a human being but also as a professional — I have to think about what people will need by the time the paper hits their driveway."

And that's a good thing, says Rachel Burrell, founder and director emeritus of Fernside, A Center for Grieving Children. "In many ways, we still live in a death-denying culture in this country. That Jim is brave enough to say what he does helps the community to grieve, gives us permission to grieve," she says. "They are very powerful pieces."

" ..... AS YOU FORGAVE THOSE WHO TRESPASSED AGAINST YOU. "

November 15, 1996
Cardinal Joseph Bernardin was accused of child molestation by a man who later recognized his memory as flawed.
Throughout the ordeal, Cardinal Bernardin was clear, firm and forgiving in maintaining his innocence — a real inspiration.

REST IN PEACE, JOHN-JOHN

July 20, 1999
When a prominent person dies, I scan for memorable images from his or her life that may help tell that individual's story.

February 1, 1987
Cincinnati's annual Christmas confrontation with the Klan cross leaves us frustrated.
Thankfully, Martin Luther King Day follows soon afterward as a symbol of ultimate triumph over hatred and division.

"HE WANTS TO KNOW, 'CAN YOU GET USED TO WRITING THE MAJORITY OPINION?'..."

January 27, 1993
I enjoyed slyly implying that liberals rule in heaven. Thurgood Marshall deserved as much
after rowing against the current throughout his tenure on the Supreme Court.

September 6, 1997
It felt jarring to draw God as a small, poor, Third World child, but it may be a more
compelling image than the white-bearded Old Testament figure.

June 10, 1982
How does a peanut vendor become a beloved figure to an entire city? Seeing Peanut Jim Shelton outside
Crosley Field was somehow as exciting as that first glimpse of infield grass through the tunnels.

December 16, 1999
I had spent a day with Charles Schulz in his studio in Santa Rosa, CA, about a year before he died. He was a complex man, amazingly generous, but with an overwhelming sense of sadness about him. This drawing was made when he announced his retirement.

...BUT DELIVER US FROM EVIL. AMEN.

December 14, 1997
Drawn after Cincinnati police officers Ronald Jeter and Daniel Pope were gunned down
one awful night, copies of this were mailed to every police officer who requested one.

IN THOSE DAYS
THERE WERE GIANTS...

TED BERRY
1905-2000

October 18, 2000
His family asked for this drawing, which I feel is inadequate thanks for his leadership and courage.

GOODNIGHT, DR. SEUSS

September 27, 1991
I watercolored this drawing and it hangs in my daughter's room. Ted Geisel
was no less brilliant as a cartoonist than he was as a writer.

January 29, 1986
When the space shuttle Challenger exploded with teacher Christa McAuliffe
on board, tearful children expressed what was in our hearts.

" A MISTER ASTAIRE TO SEE YOU, BOSS......"

June 25, 1987
Some cartoon images arrive in a burst of inspiration with virtually no effort.
The only challenge is to get the image on paper before it gets away.

September 11, 2001
I heard about the attack on New York City and Washington at 10 a.m. and got a call from my editor saying the *Enquirer* would need a drawing by 11:30 a.m. for a special afternoon edition. The image would have to be simple and powerful.

...THAT OUR FLAG WAS STILL THERE
September 12, 2001
As a teen-ager, I had seen the tattered flag that flew above Fort McHenry
and inspired the *Star-Spangled Banner*. Its scars make it all the more inspiring.

JIM'S MOM TAKES A BUS TO WORK TO BUSS THE BOSS

BY CLIFF RADEL

Enquirer *Metro* columnist Radel grew up on Cincinnati's west side, attended Western Hills High School and joined the newspaper the year Jim was hired. They did not meet until they became journalism colleagues.

The first thing Jim Borgman gets when he enters his *Enquirer* office is a kiss on the cheek from his Gal Friday.

That's allowed.

She's his mother.

Marian Borgman is also Jim's confidant, his rock in times both happy and sad.

Their special, often unspoken bond grew even stronger when she started working for him on March 23, 1980.

"That was just after Jim's cartoons were first syndicated," she said, consulting a worn sheaf of rubber-band bound timesheets.

She wanted to make sure she had her starting date right.

She did.

"He tried mailing his cartoons to the newspapers by himself," she added. "But it took too much time.

"So I said, 'Do you think I could do that?' I was available. All my kids were out of the house. So, I started coming down to the *Enquirer*. Now I do it three mornings a week."

Jim's Gal Monday-Wednesday-Friday beats him to work by two hours. She's in by 7 a.m. He gets his kiss around 9.

"I don't do a whole lot," she said, exhibiting the sense of modesty that runs in her family. "Jim gets his cartoons printed up the night before. I mail them out the next morning.

"The syndicate pays me for

the postage. Jim pays me for my time."

She sat at a desk in her son's corner office. Envelopes got stuffed as she spoke.

Nineteen floors below, morning rush-hour traffic crawled along the city's cross-town connector, Fort Washington Way. Outside her window seat loomed Paul Brown Stadium. Beyond that gray and white behemoth flowed the Ohio River.

"I love seeing the river from up here," Marian Borgman said. "Water fascinates me."

But not enough to keep her from working. She stole a glance out the window. Then she went back to inserting copies of her son's cartoon into

Marian Borgman prepares copies of Jim's drawings for mailing. His work is syndicated to more than 190 publications through King Features.

envelopes for 150 newspapers across the country, from Alaska and Hawaii to Florida and Maine.

"We used to mail more than 300," she said. "But now most newspapers get their cartoons by computer."

After stuffing the envelopes, she takes an extra cartoon and glues it — centered and straight, wrinkle-free and pristine — to a piece of stiff white paper. When the glue dries, she files the mounted cartoon chronologically in a drawer with the rest of Jim's recent work.

At this point in her day, Marian Borgman lets herself take a look at Jim's latest cartoon.

Sometimes she sees people she knows in his work.

Sometimes she sees herself.

Jeremy, the star of the *Zits* comic strip Jim co-authors with Jerry Scott, occasionally lies on the porch roof outside his bedroom window when life overwhelms his teen-age coping skills.

Jim's son, Dylan, sits on the porch roof outside his bedroom window.

"The first thing Jim Borgman gets when he enters his Enquirer office is a kiss on the cheek from his Gal Friday. That's allowed."

Cliff Radel

25 THINGS TO BREAK WRITERS BLOCK

Hang around Fountain Square
Read *Mad* magazine
Listen to reggae
Turn the lights out
Fill three sketchbook pages with anything
Drive home a new way
Walk in the woods
Watch *Dumb and Dumber*
Draw with a different pen or pencil
Sit beside moving water
Talk to an old college friend
Have cereal for supper
Sketch Frisch's waitresses
Take a nap
Give up and take a walk
Sacrifice a goat
Talk to a little kid
Dinner with someone who makes me laugh
Take a long drive
Plan my retirement
Rearrange the furniture
Apply for a mail route
Go with your gut
Seek divine intervention
Get a foot massage

"He's got a little table and chair out there," Mrs. Borgman said.

"One time, Jim drove me over to his house and Jeremy, I mean Dylan, was sitting out there. Nearly scared me to half to death."

She sorted through a stack of Jim's vintage cartoons.

"That older couple," she said,

pointing to a drawing of a man and woman struggling to survive a heat wave, "could be me and Jim's dad."

The woman wore glasses. Her hair was white and curly. Just like Marian Borgman.

The man's features were tougher to make out. He had his lips wrapped around the room-cooling vents of a window air-conditioner.

Shoehorned into a bathing suit and plopped in an easy chair, the woman sat in front of a TV — her bare feet resting on a hassock — and next to a cold drink.

Fanning herself, she showed her husband no mercy.

"Oh, knock it off, Irvin," she grumped. "Everybody's hot."

Marian Borgman chuckled at the likeness. Then pointed out the dissimilarities.

"That could be me," she said. "But you won't see me laying around in a bathing suit. I don't swim. And I'm not a drinker."

Or a loafer.

Marian Borgman is an old school, west-side mom. Hard worker. Early riser. Devoted to her family. Not stuck on herself.

"I'm up every morning at 4:30," she said. "That's before the alarm goes off.

"Why sleep late? Morning's the best part of the day."

That's Cincinnati's west side talking. If you sit around, you're lazy. So get off your duff. Time's wasting. There's work to be done.

Mondays, Wednesdays and Fridays, she's out the door of her Westwood apartment by 5:50 a.m.

She drives across Western Hills to Sunset and St. Williams. She parks near St. William Church whose school was attended by Jim, his younger brother Tom and older sisters Kathy and Mary Jo. The church is just a block away from Trenton Avenue, where she raised her four children in a modest two-story brick home with her husband, Jim.

"My son Jim is not a junior," she noted. "He's James Mark. My husband was James Robert."

At 6:30 a.m., she catches the bus for town.

"I don't care to drive on the expressways. Too crowded. Too crazy."

Sitting in a side seat across from the driver, she takes the hilly ride in silence.

"I can't read on the bus. Too noisy."

The ride is smooth and short.

And very convenient. Her stop is a block away from the *Enquirer.*

"I use my cane to grab the rope to signal for my stop," she said. "Then I walk to the paper."

She takes her time. And puts her cane to work.

"I use the cane to keep my balance. Three years ago, I had hip-replacement surgery. I have osteoarthritis, and I had a sciatic nerve problem. My back gets to me every now and then. So falling is my biggest fear."

Her workday is brief. And trouble-free.

"Some days I'm finished with my work in two hours, sometimes three. I just keep working until it's done."

She must be doing something right. For decades, she's mailed Jim's work without a hitch. "So far, no one has complained about not getting a cartoon on time."

After the last envelope is stuffed and mailed, Marian Borgman kisses her son goodbye. She heads for the bus stop and home.

The outbound bus stops at Eighth and State. Marian Borgman sees a familiar place, the building where her husband spent his entire career — first as a sign painter, then as general manager of the O.H. Roth Co.

One April morning in 1984,

Jim's dad wasn't feeling well. He stayed home from work and drove himself to the hospital for tests.

Marian got a call from the hospital. Her husband had suffered a heart attack in the waiting room. She raced to be by his side. He died that afternoon.

Jim and Marian were married 38 years.

"He was so proud of Jim," she said.

"Every day Jim's cartoon was in the paper, Dad would cut it out and put it in an album. He never missed one for eight years."

Marian Borgman thought about continuing the scrapbooks.

But she decided against it.

"That," she said, "was Dad's thing."

Besides, fate had other designs on her time. Fifteen years later, she would sadly have to return to the role she once occupied as mom, the single most important woman in her son's life.

The clock atop Marian Borgman's china closet sounds its Westminster chimes every 15 minutes.

"That clock was a gift to Jim's dad," she said as she sat at her dining room table. Pride swelled in her voice as she added: "He got it when he became a Grand

"That older couple," she said, pointing to a drawing of a man and woman struggling to survive a heat wave, "could be me and Jim's dad."

Marian Borgman

Knight in the Knights of Columbus."

Patting the gleaming finish protecting the table's blond wood, she said: "The china closet and this table are part of our original dining room furniture."

The Borgmans sat down to holiday feasts and Sunday dinners at that table. Everything was made from scratch. Turkey with dressing. Pot roast. Meatloaf. Mock turtle soup. Chili. Meatballs and spaghetti. Devil's food cake for every birthday. Bowls brimming with the favorite side dish of Jim's dad, homemade apple sauce, made from tart, green Lodi apples.

Today, the table holds a jigsaw puzzle Marian Borgman is assembling.

"It's a famous photo from *Life* magazine," she said. "A bunch of steelworkers are sitting on a beam. It's called, 'Lunchtime on a Crossbeam.' I got it as a birthday gift. I just turned 79. I'm getting up there."

She laughed.

Then fell silent.

The smile faded from her face as she spoke.

"Today is Lynn's birthday," she said softly.

"She would have been 47, the same age as Jim."

Lynn Borgman died in 1999, suddenly and unexpectedly of a

> *"But I'm proud of him the way he's carried on with his work and with the way he's raising his children, Chelsea and Dylan."*
> **Marian Borgman**

25 REJECTED TITLES FOR *ZITS*

Jeremy
Jeremy's World
Jeremy and Stuff
Stuff
Stuff About Me
Whatever
Why Me?
Why Not?
Chill
Back Off
Duh
Work in Progress
Yo
Grounded
Grounded for Life
Crossroads
On My Case
Get Off My Case
Planet Jeremy
As If!
Cowboy
Supposedly My Life
Chad and Jeremy
Life and Stuff
Deal With It

blood clot after undergoing surgery to ease chronic neck and shoulder pain.

Her tragic death shattered Jim's world.

"He'd come into the office and try to work," his mother recalled. "All of a sudden, he'd get up, close his door and break down."

Through his tears, he'd ask:

"How long does this go on?"

She'd answer: "It's just something you have to get through."

Then she'd wrap her arms around her sobbing son.

"Somehow," she said, "he got through it.

"He still misses Lynn terribly. And he always will.

"But I'm proud of him the way he's carried on with his work and with the way he's raising his children, Chelsea and Dylan."

Just thinking about it, she said, makes her start to cry.

And she wiped her eyes.

Changing the subject to a happier topic, she said:

"Let me show you my treasures."

One framed work of art by each of her children hangs on her walls.

Jim's caricature of his dad.

Tom's watercolor of the men of the family.

Mary Jo's embroidery of marigolds.

Kathy's dried flower arrangement.

"I'm proud of all of my children," Marian Borgman said, leading the tour through her apartment's art gallery.

"I won't show partiality to any of my kids. To me, they're all great."

But the one she gets to kiss three mornings a week is Jim.

A Salute From A Colleague

Several of Jim's professional colleagues were asked to commemorate his silver anniversary at The Enquirer. *This drawing was created by Signe Wilkinson, Pulitzer Prize winning cartoonist of* The Philadelphia *Daily News.*

SO WHERE AM I TAKING YOU TODAY?

JIM TAKING HIS MUSE FOR A WALK

"MY OLDEST WAS AN ALL-NATURAL DELIVERY.... THEN FREDDY WAS CAESAREAN .... JENNY WAS IN VITRO...... AND THE TWINS CAME FREEZE-DRIED IN THEIR OWN RESEALABLE ZIP-LOCK STORAGE BAGS."

August 20, 1989
Medical miracles bring us new life in novel ways each day.
Sometimes you can't imagine what could be next.

"DON'T TAKE IT PERSONALLY, WALTER..... A LOT OF PEOPLE GET A CASE OF THE BLAHS THIS TIME OF YEAR."

January 24, 1997
As February approaches each year, I find it a real challenge.
My spirit goes flat as the gray of the skies. Drawing helps me deal with the gray days.

" .... AND THIS, MR. SECRETARY, IS OUR PROCUREMENT STAFF...... COMMANDER CURLY, ADMIRAL LARRY AND GENERAL MOE. "

March 11, 1985

Casper Weinberger's term as secretary of defense was the era of $600 toilet seats and $500 hammers. When Cap retired, I drew him receiving a gold watch from President Reagan and exclaiming, "This must have cost billions!"

June 3, 1994
A lot of graduates thanked their parents with this diploma,
which the *Enquirer* made available when requests poured in.

December 2, 1997
Drawing *Zits* keeps me thinking like a teen-ager. The closer I look, the more I'm heartened by the teen-agers
I know, particularly because their temptations and challenges can be overwhelming.

"IMAGINE THE NOIVE!!.......... THEY WANT A SEVEN-YEAR EXTENSION!"

July 16, 1978
When I began at the *Enquirer* in 1976, green and politically unformed, it was assumed that I would fall into line with the
Enquirer's editorial philosophy. This was one of my first outright breaks from the prevailing editorial policy..

"OH, KNOCK IT OFF, IRVIN ...... EVERYBODY'S HOT..."

July 15, 1986
Those of us in the media dread summers, when the news slows down and the heat is the only thing on anyone's mind.

January 14, 1996
Hillary Clinton changed hairstyles the way her husband changed his policy positions.
This one must have followed a scalping by Sen. Alphonse D'Amato over health care..

THE HOSTILE TAKEOVER

September 18, 1988
Certain terms creep into our language without much explanation: stem cells, missile shield,
softening economy, pop-up showers. The more colorful the language, the more my mind wanders.

"INTERESTING.....IT'S LIKE A PORTABLE 500K FILE *and* YOU DON'T HAVE TO WAIT FOR IT TO DOWNLOAD.... AND YOU SAY IT'S CALLED A NEWSPAPER?"

August 1, 1997
Sometimes the greatest technological marvels are lying in our driveways each morning.

THE PEACEABLE KINGDOM

January 16, 1980
This is my first syndicated editorial cartoon. King Features had recently signed me to
provide four cartoons a week to a list of about 70 newspapers. I was terrified.

July 19, 1998
Gulp! Pure autobiography.

PLANETS LINE UP TO CREATE NEW COMIC STRIP STAR

BY JERRY SCOTT

Jerry Scott lives in California and spends at least one hour each day on the phone with Jim Borgman brainstorming Zits.

An astrologer, two cartoonists and a rabbi walk into a restaurant. Stop me if you've heard this.

This is a chronicle of the days leading up to and including the creation of *Zits*. Well, maybe chronicle is too strong of a word to use here. Chronicles tend to be fairly factual, and I'm not sure this can carry that guarantee. As a cartoonist, my job involves spending a lot of time inside my own head rewriting and editing the actual events of my life to be used for publication later. Because of this, the polished versions of my memories tend to be much more concise, provocative and entertaining than the raw material would ever

suggest. Forget "chronicle." Let's just call it an essay.

With that in mind, picture a morning in the spring of 1996 when Jim Borgman telephoned me to say he had been invited to speak to a group of journalists in Phoenix. I was living in a ragged little town called Cave Creek, just north of Scottsdale, and Jim was calling to get my advice on where he could burn off a couple of days in Arizona. The speaking engagement was going to take up only a couple of hours, and he would have come too far just to turn around and fly back to Cincinnati that evening or even the next morning.

I told him about a place I love called Garland's in Sedona, about

an hour and a half north of Phoenix. It's a small resort with tidy little cabins. It serves enormous breakfasts and fancy gourmet dinners with words on the menu like "boeuf" instead of beef, in a rustic stone and timber lodge that would have made the Cartwright boys feel at home. This is just the type of place where a guy can get away all by himself and not think about work.

So, naturally, I invited myself along. And I brought work. Not work-work, but a handful of sketches of a new comic strip I'd been working on about a teen-age boy, which I was very happy with, except for the drawings.

Jim and I were just casual friends at the time. We were

JERRY SCOTT and JIM BORGMAN

The strip at top was Jerry Scott's vision of the comic strip before he collaborated with Jim. The strip at the bottom shows Jim's influence on Zits and, especially, Jeremy.

serving together on the board of directors of the National Cartoonists Society, and the longest conversation I can remember our having before this was inside a crippled airplane on the tarmac of Hartsfield International Airport in Atlanta.

We had accidentally run into each other in the boarding area of a late-afternoon connecting flight to Sarasota, Fla., on our way to one of those very board meetings. As the plane was backing away from the gate, there was a loud pop, and the plane lurched to a stop. We watched the pilot wrestle the spare out of the trunk and search for the jack until we got bored, and for the next couple of hours just talked about stuff like politics, marriage, kids, religion and comics. At the time, a two-hour delay on a sweltering airport runway seemed like a real nuisance, but now I'm beginning to realize how much we owe that defective tire.

Sedona was beautiful, as it always is, and by the second

otherwise, it's not easy to ask Jim Borgman for a critique of your artwork. Next to his, my drawings look goofy. In fact, next to his, almost everybody's drawings look goofy; and not the good goofy, either. The bad, clumsy, humiliating kind of goofy that makes you want to

sketchbook shut. "It's funny, isn't it?"

"Yes," I said. "But the drawings — they're all wrong. They look like they were drawn by the guy who does Nancy and Sluggo."

"True enough," he agreed solemnly.

"What do you think I should do?" I ventured. "How would you draw a teen-ager?"

In my 46 years of life, I've never actually heard the angels sing, but that day, on that cabin porch, along Oak Creek among the sycamores above Sedona, Arizona, I think I may have at least heard them hum a few notes. Jim picked up his pen and scribbled a quick sketch of a teen-age boy, and time stopped. I immediately knew that a strip about teen-agers would have to be drawn with a loose, gritty style like Jim's. And the main character should be 15 (not 13 or 14, as I had drawn him), and not in a million years would I ever be able to come close to drawing something with as much life and spontaneity as existed in that one little sketch I was staring at. No, if this was going to become a comic strip, Jim would have to draw it.

But that presented a set of problems of its own.

First, neither of us especially wanted to work with a partner. I was already working with a

DRAWING BOARD STRETCHES 2000 MILES

Although all of the drawings for *Zits* are still done with good old-fashioned ink on paper, the transmission of ideas and art between us relies heavily on the fax machine, the telephone and the Internet. It still amazes us sometimes that we can create this comic strip together across 2000 miles of desert, mountains, prairie and cornfields.

The nuts and bolts of the process goes like this: I write the majority of the material, supported by Jim's ideas and suggestions and around an hour's worth of conversation with him every morning. Then I draw pencil sketches of the strips and fax them to his studio

at home, usually in batches of six or 12. Jim then puts his own spin on the gags and redraws the strips in pencil before faxing them back to me. We then go over each panel carefully, reading them aloud and fine-tuning the dialogue, drawings and especially the characters' facial expressions.

After we're both satisfied with the result, Jim then inks the strips, scans them and e-mails them off to the syndicate.

The Sunday strips work pretty much the same way, except that Jim colors them on the computer before sending them off.

afternoon we were pretty hiked-out and ready to just sit around a little. I remembered the comic-strip-in-progress that I'd brought along, and decided to run it by Jim.

So I ambled over to his cabin with a couple of beers, my sketchbook and a knot in my stomach. In case you think

throw your own work in a deep hole and look for another career.

But I handed him the sketches anyway and took a deep, cleansing swig of beer. Naturally, Jim was polite and read every one of the strips, even chuckling in the appropriate places.

"So what's the problem with it?" he asked, flipping the

partner, Rick Kirkman, on *Baby Blues,* and was focused on the idea of doing a second strip on my own. I just write *Baby Blues,* and I missed the drawing part of cartooning. In fact, I'm not even sure that you can call yourself a cartoonist if you don't actually draw anything. And you're not exactly a real writer, either, if, like me, all you write is dialogue and sound effects (Hey! What th—? POW! (GASP!) FRAAP!).

Second, Jim had just ended his syndicated politics comic strip, *Wonk City,* and wasn't really interested in giving up the nights, weekends, vacations and holidays for another shot at obscurity.

Third, the odds of a new comic strip succeeding these days are astronomical. How could we even think of committing to a project like this if we didn't know what the future held? We needed a sign. We continued to talk, anyway, about teen-agers, and comics, and comics about teen-agers, for the rest of the afternoon and right up until dinnertime.

There's just one seating for dinner at Garland's, and it's done family-style, often with total strangers sitting together at fairly large tables. That evening we found ourselves across from a tall, gaunt man with an aggressive beard and gentle eyes. Next to him sat his wife, an intelligent-looking woman in her late 30s. She wore a broad-brimmed black hat, wire-rimmed glasses and a thoughtful smile. They introduced themselves as David and Bonnie from Mesa, Arizona, and the small talk began.

"How do you do? Have you been here before? Yes, we have been coming here for 14 years. Interesting! Mesa, huh? What do you do there?

"Well, I'm an astrologer and Bonnie here is a rabbi."

Stunned silence.

In retrospect, I wish we would have asked Bonnie more questions about her job, but instead, we did what most people probably do when they find themselves across a table from this particular couple — we started asking the astrologer to predict the future.

Not wanting to offend the guy (or agitate the beard), we listened politely and pretended to believe him when he flipped through that little dog-eared book of his and said the stars were telling him that Jim and I would make a good team. That since we were cartoonists, a comic strip we might create together would be a phenomenal success. That such a collaboration would redefine our careers. That our planets (by this time, the astrologer was standing on his chair) were aligned in such a precise and remarkable way that it would be an affront to all things astrological if we didn't take this opportunity and work together on this project.

So, to keep peace in the heavens, we did.

At least that's the way I remember it happening this time.

A SALUTE FROM A COLLEAGUE

Several of Jim's professional colleagues were asked to commemorate his silver anniversary at The Enquirer. *This drawing was created by Jerry Scott, Jim's partner in the comic strip* Zits *and the co-author of the comic strip* Baby Blues.

Chapter 14

COFFEE AND CONVERSATION WITH JAMES MARK BORGMAN

BY JIM KNIPPENBERG

Enquirer *Tempo* columnist Jim Knippenberg is a west sider and a graduate of Elder High School, Jim Borgman's alma mater.

Jim Borgman was looking like the old cliche. You know the one, the wide-eyed deer in the headlights.

"101 questions? I don't think I know 101 answers," he said, looking all the more pale in contrast to the bright purple shirt he was wearing.

But that was the plan: Drag him out of the office, sit him down, make nice awhile, then ambush him with 101 fill-in-the-blanks ranging from dead serious to off-the-wall to, well, just plain nosy.

And so we did. 3 p.m. on a sunny Tuesday, sitting at a picnic table outside the *Enquirer's* lobby. Three cups of coffee, two large chocolate chip cookies, one potty break, a dozen interruptions and four hours later, we had 101 answers.

Ready?

"Go ahead."

The highlight of my career . . .

No question, it was seeing my cartoon framed above Clinton's john in the Oval Office. I understand I'm framed over a lot of people's johns. Jeeze, life just doesn't get any better than that, does it?

My mentor's best advice to me . . .

Chuck Jones, an animator for Warner Bros., was a wise and wonderful mentor. He called right after I won the Pulitzer and said, 'You have the power to make people happy. You must use it.'

The only thing better than the Pulitzer would be . . .

Winning the Nobel. But I don't think they give it for cartooning. Maybe I could switch to a career in physics.

I'll leave Cincinnati when . . .

I never told myself I'd stay here forever, but as the years march on, it gets harder and harder to picture what would make me want to leave. I have a wonderful life and perfect job. The paper lets me say what I want, and that's the main thing a cartoonist looks for. The freedom to be an independent voice.

Raising two teen-agers alone is like . . .

Oh, I don't think I'm raising them alone. I have support from all sides — family, friends, a wonderful nanny. I don't feel alone at all.

I'm too critical of . . .

Almost everything. As a perfectionist and a contrarian, I'm always trying to find that one nit to pick. The biggest target, of course, is always myself.

I'm not critical enough of . . .

I'm drawing a blank. Oh, I know, movies. I tend to like them all, even the ones that get two stars. I have really low standards.

Music hath charm to . . .

Get me through a lot of boring times. After I get an idea (for a cartoon), I turn on music and slip into the zone and don't look up until hours later. When I have an intricate drawing that requires a lot of problem solving, I play classical music. When it's one where I know from the start where I'm going, I play something more lively. Springsteen, maybe.

The outdoor activity I'll never give up . . .

I like to ride my bike. I'm afraid of cars in this city, since they don't give much room to bicycles, so I usually go to Winton Woods or Miami Whitewater.

The three foods I'd have to take to a desert island . . .

Salmon (and a grill), an assortment of veggies, also to grill, and something Indian. Maybe tandoori chicken. And if you'll let me have a fourth, it would be salsa. I guess I could always smuggle it on, too.

When I just can't come up with an idea . . .

I usually go to Starbucks and wait for the caffeine to kick in. When the idea isn't there, you just gotta get away from the drawing board and move around. I get a lot of ideas in this alley (Ogden Place), just walking to Starbucks.

I have this hobby and it's . . .

I don't, really. As close as it comes is reading with the kids. Chelsea and I read every night —

we've powered our way through Harry Potter, *Watership Down, The Hobbit*, lots of young adult fiction.

Politically, I'm . . .

A contrarian is what I prefer. In this town, I'm seen as a flaming liberal, but outside this city I'd be seen as a moderate. Even conservative when it comes to my blue-collar values. My dad was a sign painter, for heaven's sake. I still feel the hairs on the back of my neck stand up when people start talking about entitlement. And then that feeling does battle with a fundamental sense of compassion.

Organized religion is . . .

People who have a church talk about it like it's a second home. I envy that. I haven't found that in my life yet.

Cincinnati's racial strife is . . .

Well, I believe this is a good-hearted city. But we're at a moment in time when we're looking for someone to get us to the next level. Frankly, I don't see anyone who can do it. I really don't feel like we have yet walked a mile in each other's shoes and that's something we need to do.

Local politics are . . .

Pathetic. Humorous. Ridiculous. Cartoonable. They certainly make my job easier.

Daily newspapering is . . .

An aerobic sport with no time to rest. I compare it to this little animal I saw on a National Geographic special — the pygmy shrew scurries along the riverbank and has to eat the equivalent of its body weight every hour. I think that's a perfect metaphor for newspapers.

The hardest part of working on *Zits* . . .

The fact that there aren't 28 hours in a day. I usually work on it at night, after the kids go to bed, and it really is very therapeutic. I love taking stuff from life and putting it through the cartoon mill. It turns your biggest trials and tribulations into a cartoon idea. But working with Jerry (Scott,

Chuck Jones, an animator for Warner Bros., was a wise and wonderful mentor. He called right after I won the Pulitzer and said, 'You have the power to make people happy. You must use it.'

The truth is, I can't stand parties. I like people one-on-one, or maybe two. I don't like a room full of people. Also, I can't stand public speaking and that's unfortunate. I'm OK and I enjoy it once I get going, but I'm in agony building up to it. I don't really like the spotlight.

co-creator), well, I love our relationship.

I like clothes that . . .

Fit loose and are colorful. But you know, they don't make many colorful clothes for big guys like me, short of Hawaiian shirts that make me look like some kind of big ole flag.

I'm most creative when . . .

I'm just a little too busy. That's a fine line — you don't want to be extremely busy because that locks you up. But also, if I'm not busy at all, then my mind wanders off into the nowhere zone.

I'm least creative when . . .

I'm overwhelmed.

Cars are . . .

I'm one of the few guys born without a car gene. I don't know what they're all about, and I don't know a Lexus from a Yugo. To me, they're just four wheels with a motor that makes them roll when you need to go somewhere.

When I retire . . .

I'd love to hang around the Southwest a lot. I can't get enough of that big sky.

I'm healthy, but . . .

I'm aging. I have all these middle-age whiney things that everyone else has — my knees hurt, I'm leakier and gassier than I'd like to be. Is this too much information? Are you sorry you asked?

(Trying to gross us out, 'eh? Maybe get out of this session early? It's not going to work. Keep talking.)

My dad . . .

Was a sign painter in Price Hill with four kids. Unlike other men of his generation, he was a very present father. One of my fondest memories is that he would bring home signs to paint in the garage at night. After we all got our pajamas on, we'd go down to say good night, and I'd sit there and watch him paint the letters. I used to love to watch it take shape and try to figure out what it was going to say as he went along. He died in '84.

My mom . . .

She works with me, I don't know if people

know that. I've gotten to know her better since my dad died. She had always been the steady, quiet one. She's my hero.

When I think of Elder High School . . .

Elder was good for me. I found my circle — kids who were creative and wanted to be challenged. I never felt much in tune with the athletic aspect, which is what most people think when they think of Elder, but I did find my sub-groups. Plus it has a great art program.

I get embarrassed when . . .

I have to dress up. I don't think I look right in ties and coats. I feel like I look more like a float in a Macy's Thanksgiving Parade.

_____ always amazes me . . .

My children. Always. I'm thinking of earlier in their lives, when you know everything that goes into their ears. Then as they grow into lives outside your house, you find them always bringing home something new. I love a houseful of kids.

Museums are . . .

Great on rainy days. The very best place to be on a rainy day.

Life isn't a cabaret, old chum, it's . . .

More like a patchwork quilt, I think. At least, that's the way it strikes me.

Roller coasters are . . .

There's almost no amusement park ride I can ride and keep my last meal. Roller coasters are especially tough on my inner ear.

What I like best about baseball . . .

Is just having it on as audio wallpaper when I draw at night. I can't tell you who's winning or losing, but I love having it on. I always think it's so sad when the last game of the season hits. Oh, and I love baseball cards. I still have them all — cardboard suitcases full — because my mom never threw them away. They're pretty battered and tattered by now.

When I just gotta dance . . .

I never gotta dance. I've been taking dance

lessons — sort of jazzy ballet — for more than a year, but I never really get airborne. I really have no rhythm at all. I think I'm terminally white.

The best antidote for grief . . .

Is time. But until enough time has passed, the best antidote is good friends. I have the most amazing support system — I'm surrounded by people who are willing to care for me.

I think prayer is . . .

Fundamental to staying balanced. I prefer free-form prayer, usually in an urgent tone of voice.

I can't stand . . .

These are hard questions. Am I starting to sound like a Playmate of the Month or something?

The truth is, I can't stand parties. I like people one-on-one, or maybe two. I don't like a room full of people. Also, I can't stand public speaking and that's unfortunate. I'm OK and I enjoy it once I get going, but I'm in agony building up to it. I don't really like the spotlight.

My Mac is . . .

It's, um, well, I'm not technologically sharp. My kids can run rings around me. But within the ways I use it, my Mac is enjoyable. I use it to color my cartoons and I enjoy that process. And e-mail — I like e-mail a lot. Much better than phone calls. They're so intrusive and not welcome in my life because they always ring when I'm in the middle of something. E-mail lets you communicate on your own terms.

One president I'd like to see come back . . .

That would have to be Nixon. Or maybe Clinton. Both were bigger than life, colorful, multifaceted personalities that were fun to watch.

One president I never want to see come back . . .

George Bush the first. Drawing him was like getting blood from a turnip. What I look for is a strong personality with an expressive face and strong opinions. But the bland ones — you work forever and never feel like you're moving.

The easiest person to draw . . .

Marge Schott. Jerry Dowling (a fellow artist) and I used to have a contest to see who could get the most cigarettes in bodily orifices — mouth, ears, nose. With Marge, you just put the pen down and it draws her.

Technology has changed my art . . .

In a number of ways. I'm not on the leading edge by any means, but I've learned to color on the Mac, file a cartoon digitally, even e-mail them, and answer readers. Before that, the fax let me work from remote places. And before the fax, when I was away, I'd run all over town looking for the nearest FedEx office.

I love to shop at . . .

Bookstores like Joseph-Beth. I also like poking around World Market, and I'm really big on Costco. It's like a Sam's. But mostly I like bookstores. I always wind up buying an arm load that then sit by my bed forever.

The funniest person I ever met . . .

Bob Beemon, the art teacher at Elder. He was my best buddy in high school, too. He has such a great, fast, lively mind that half of the time I'm with him I spend laughing. Even now, he still does drawings that make me laugh.

One person whose talent I really envy . . .

I'd have to say Bruce Springsteen because of his uncanny ability to capture life as it appears to me. He's my strongest non-cartooner influence.

My friends are . . .

More than generous to me. It's almost impossible to say how big they are. I used to feel that no man is an island, but I thought I was pretty close. That was arrogance. At that point in my life I hadn't even been set back yet. In recent years, my friends have held me together.

If I had to wear just one color the rest of my life . . .

It would be purple. It's funny, both my high school and college color was purple. But I wonder,

Bob Beemon, the art teacher at Elder. He was my best buddy in high school, too. He has such a great, fast, lively mind that half of the time I'm with him I spend laughing. Even now, he still does drawings that make me laugh.

big guys like me in purple????

When I need a cocktail, it's a . . .

Margarita with a little bit of salt. It represents vacation to me. I like drinks with umbrellas and straws and cherries.

Lawyers are . . .

Not a big part of my life, thankfully. I've never been sued, knock on wood, so I've always managed to dodge the legal bullet.

Doctors are . . .

I don't know why this is, but a lot of my friends are doctors.

Nuns are . . .

There are two answers. Nuns today are the most admirable people. They go into war-torn, famine-ridden countries and feed the hungry. That inspires me. They're apart from the nuns who schooled me with sparks flying from their mouths.

Priests are . . .

The best priest I ever knew was my uncle, Gene Maly. He was dean of Mount St. Mary's (seminary) and a real intellect. They even sent him to Rome for the second Vatican Council. Growing up in Price Hill, I didn't see a lot of adventurous lives around me. He provided that bridge and the inspiration that you can get there from here.

TV's greatest strength . . .

Is animated cartoons. That's not a very good answer, but hey, I'm a cartoonist.

For local radio, I like . . .

I'm an NPR guy all the way — 'VXU and 'GUC. I wake up to Morning Edition every day.

News reporters are . . .

Great sources for me and very helpful in telling me if I'm on the right track. Anymore, they're funny to see because they look more like junior executives. I know I could work at home if I wanted, but I like their company too much.

Cops are . . .

Having a tough time right now. It's the one profession I'd be absolutely worst at of anything I

They make good material. There's nothing better than drawing a pure middle-aged guy in a flannel shirt squeezed into jeans with an 8-inch too small waist. Of which I'm one.

can think of. So I admire and appreciate what they do.

If peace breaks out . . .

I'll have to sit around all day drawing the weather.

For vacations, I like . . .

We like at least one adventure vacation a year. By that I mean a discovery vacation somewhere we've never been. Also, we return each year to two places we really love for a week at a time. I go into a 100-percent vacation mode the minute I get there.

If my pets could talk . . .

Ooooh, we have three dogs and I'm not even a dog person. They'd tell you about the evil Jim who takes his frustrations out on them. That's probably why they poop on my carpet. It's a vicious love-hate relationship.

My daily routine . . .

There isn't a lot of routine in my life and that's bad because I like routine. Monday, Wednesday and Friday I'm in the office and that's sort of a routine. Tuesday and Thursday are my flex time. Other than that, there aren't many rigid rules. One rule is that I call Jerry for about an hour a day every day to share ideas for *Zits*. Reading with Chelsea at night is sort of a routine, and Starbucks, well, that's a morning routine.

I think exercise . . .

Makes me better. Damn it! I'm never more fully awake and alive than when I'm biking or walking. Or during my twice-a-week workout routines.

My favorite Cincinnati view . . .

I would say it's from the church (Immaculata) in Mount Adams. But I also love it when people come to town and I can take them across the river on the Anderson Ferry. It's such a quaint little piece of history in the middle of the city.

Price Hill is . . .

The source of many of my drawings — those

big, doughy people sitting in their houses talking about the news as it has filtered down to them — they're based on people I knew growing up in Price Hill.

If they took down the sauerkraut curtain . . .

We'd have to seal it back up. I know I was 21 before I ever set eyes on Hyde Park Square, and I know people who have lived here all their lives and have never been west of City Hall.

One thing about my kids . . .

Is their strength and their resilience. And their creativity, Dylan in both the visual arts and in his writing, and Chelsea in her writing. I do believe they're going to do great things.

Lynn was . . .

A fabulous partner. Warm, three times as smart as me and unconditionally loving. She was a really good poet, too. She discovered quilting in the last five years of her life, so she left us with a houseful of colorful fabric. She had such great zest for life, and that broadened me. She took me by the hand and showed me the world.

The teacher who influenced me most . . .

Martin Garhart — my art professor at Kenyon. He took me from a kid who could draw things to understanding how to express myself in work. How to talk about the world in drawings. A great guy.

If I were to be a sneak couple with anyone, it would be . . .

Julia Roberts. I love that big smile and how she laughs. Or maybe Katie Couric. Warm people who laugh a lot turn me on.

As an athlete, I'm . . .

Not! I played baseball and football in grade school, but by the time I got to high school, the others were way beyond me. My most athletic feat was a dog sledding trip across Alaska. 300 miles!

Cincinnati chili is . . .

I guess a secret vice of mine. About once every two months I need it. Really need it.

Ice cream is . . .

Ooooh, Chelsea and I go get Graeter's on a lot of summer nights. It's a fun little social outing. I like toffee chip.

One thing I'll say for Cincinnati Germans . . .

They make good material. There's nothing better than drawing a pure middle-aged guy in a flannel shirt squeezed into jeans with an 8-inch too small waist. Of which I'm one.

One comedian who always makes me laugh . . .

Billy Crystal and, I hate to say it, Jim Carrey. And Steven Wright. I think Steven would be the best of the lot.

I think Kentucky . . .

Has the best views of Cincinnati. Kentucky people are very genuine and I like that — very honest and down to earth, very friendly.

What makes me angriest . . .

You mean apart from our editorial page? Just kidding. Seriously, I guess closed-mindedness. I see life as a big unfolding dialogue, so there's very little that I've drawn that I think of as a final pronouncement. When people don't understand that spirit of debate, I don't know what to do.

As an employee, my mom . . .

You couldn't get a better person to work with — she practically opens the building in the morning. Her work's pretty much finished when I get here at 9. But she is constitutionally well organized, so the job fits her perfectly. It's hard, maybe impossible, for me to be that organized. When she first started, I though omigod, what if she doesn't work out? How do I fire my own mother? But the truth is, she has worked out beautifully. It's a joy to see her every day.

Opera is . . .

Pretty challenging to me. About every two or three years I decide to try again. Several hours into it, I remember why I don't go.

Those Wagnerian sopranos wear tin

Martin Garhart — my art professor at Kenyon. He took me from a kid who could draw things to understanding how to express myself in work. How to talk about the world in drawings. A great guy.

25 CURIOUS BORGMAN FACTS

I can't draw a person yawning without yawning the whole time myself.

Ryan White's mother had the drawing of Ryan's arrival in heaven carved onto his gravestone.

My Uncle Gene was the dean of Mount St. Mary's Seminary.

Outside the United States, *Zits* is most popular in Sweden, Finland and Estonia.

Both of my grandmothers passed away on the same day, my sister's 21st birthday.

Charlton Heston once traded me a signed movie script for an original.

I once found myself at a lecture on an obscure species of bats with Al Gore.

Though I always draw myself holding a crow quill pen, I draw almost exclusively with a brush.

The most exotic thing I ever did was mush a dogsled across the northern coast of Alaska.

The second most exotic thing I ever did was wear brown socks with a blue suit.

After hundreds of talks I've given, public speaking still makes me physically ill.

My parents let me paint my bedroom black in 1968, God bless 'em.

I won the *Enquirer's* first Pulitzer Prize on the 150th birthday of the newspaper.

I have never been sued over a cartoon.

A guy did once threaten to mine my yard, however.

I have never been convicted of a felony beyond a reasonable doubt.

I didn't learn that it was Jim Borgman Day in Cincinnati until 7pm of that day, so I wasted like 19 hours of it.

Tom Borgman, my brother, is the creative director at the *St. Louis Post-Dispatch*.

My all-time record is four editorial cartoons in a day, though two is usually a struggle.

Zits is typically drawn between 10pm and 2am.

My son is the only person who has ever made me shoot lemonade out my nose.

Borgman originals are owned by Jimmy Carter, Hillary Clinton, Susan Stamberg, Ronald Reagan, Steven Spielberg, Dan Rather, Norman Schwarzkopf, Susan Butcher, Bill Clinton and John Updike.

Every editorial cartoon I've ever had published outside of the *Enquirer* was mailed, faxed or FedExed by my mother.

My sketchbooks will never be displayed in a glass case in a museum with one page turned each day. They're virtually indecipherable.

I still have my old baseball cards.

brassieres because . . .
I imagine they get a lot of stuff thrown at them. But they make a wonderful metaphor for cartoonists.

Camping out is . . .
I had one memorable experience in Wyoming. I was with a friend who knew how to survive. Thank God. He baby-sat me the whole time or I would have been dead. It was thrilling, but killing.

All neckties should be . . .
Safely home in their closets. If you're going to wear one, at least do one that's colorful and interesting. When I dress up, I always joke that I have to have the tie back to Skeffington's by the next day.

If I were a photographer, I'd shoot . . .
Western landscapes. All Ansel Adams stuff. All the time.

Modern medicine . . .
I feel like I have so many friends who are surviving harrowing health crises that would have killed them 10 years ago. So I think it's awesome. It's also leading us into interesting ethical places, what with the manipulation of human life. When and how much?

Telephones should be . . .
I wouldn't just ban cell phones. I'd ban them all. No more than one in 10 calls I get is really welcome. They're so derailing of any train of thought you have going. I need long stretches of being in the zone to do my work. Uninterrupted stretches.

Newsrooms are . . .
Fun. Exciting. Charged. Lots of colorful characters, full of smart people. People who want to be on the edge of what's going on. I love election night or when a really big story is in the air.

Airports are . . .
Kind of lonely, aren't they? Always about